Editorial Director. . . . . Lisa Bearnson

Editor. . . . . Tracy White

Copy Editors . . . . Jana Lillie, Kim Sandoval

Editorial Assistant . . . . Rachael Stone

Art Director. . . . . Don Lambson

Designer . . . . Joleen Hughes

Production Designers . . . . Amy Tippetts, Exposure Graphics

Publisher . . . . Mark Seastrand

Marketing Director . . . . Valerie Dellastatious

Production Manager . . . . Tom Stuber

Wholesale Accounts 800/815-3538

. . . . Stores A–O ext. 235, Stores P–Z ext. 226

Advertising. . Jenny Grothe, Debbie Hanni, Barbara Tanner, RaNay Winter

- -

Cover photo © Tom and DeeAnn McCarthy/The Stock Market

- -

For information on obtaining permission for reprints and excerpts, please contact Jessica Stevenson at *Creating Keepsakes* magazine in Orem, Utah, at 801/224-8235 ext. 227. For information on ordering *Creating Keepsakes* magazine, call 888/247-5282.

NOTICE OF LIABILITY

TRADEMARKS

THE **BIG IDEA BOOK** OF
BABY MEMORIES

Over **360** *Scrapbook Pages*

for the New Kid

on the Block

Porch Swing Publishing, Inc.

P.O. Box 469007

Escondido, California 92046

Toll-free number: 888/247-5282

International: 760/745-2809

CONTENTS

"The Light of Our Lives" *Page by Karen Glenn of Orem, Utah.* **Supplies** *Pen:* Zig Opaque Writer, EK Success; *Sun, stars, clouds and moons:* Karen's own designs.

"This Little Light of Mine" *Page by Genevieve Glassy of Tenino, Washington.* **Supplies** *Patterned paper:* Paper Adventures; *Punches:* Family Treasures (small and medium circle); Emagination (small sun); All Night Media (mini-sun, mini-star); Memories Forever (small star); *Hole punch:* Memories Forever; *Alphabet letters:* Repositionable Sticky Die-Cut Letters, Provo Craft; *Pens:* Gelly Roll and Micron Pigma, Sakura.

ON THE COVER "Micah Loves . . ." *Page by Angelyn Bryce of West Chester, Pennsylvania.* **Supplies** *Patterned paper:* Close To My Heart/D.O.T.S.; *Computer font:* Source unknown; *Lettering template:* Rounded, Pebble Tracers, Pebbles in my Pocket; *Pen:* Zig Writer, EK Success; *Bananas:* Angelyn's own designs.

MORE DELIVERIES

BOOKS

❶ *The Art of Creative Lettering*
—by Becky Higgins and Siobhan McGowan

Easy instructions for making amazing alphabets for scrapbook pages, greeting cards, invitations, and signs. Features:

- 50 brand-new, never-before-published creative lettering alphabets
- More than 300 color illustrations
- Illustrated "Lettering Toolbox" section

128 pages for $19.95, paperback
$25.00, hardcover

❷ *Mom's Little Book of Photo Tips*
—by Lisa Bearnson and Siobhan McGowan

Are you the family photographer? *Mom's Little Book of Photo Tips* celebrates that moms are very often the ones behind the camera. This non-technical advice book is packed with:

- 75 idea-oriented tips about composition, lighting, and setting up fun shots
- More than 180 great pictures by non-professional photographers who happen to be moms
- Ideas for using your point-and-shoot camera; no special equipment needed!

96 pages for $16.95, hardcover

SPECIAL ISSUES

❸ *Heritage Scrapbooks*

Remember when doors were left unlocked, and children drank soda from the icebox and the good guys always won? Come travel back in time with *Creating Keepsakes'* new idea book *Heritage Scrapbooks*. Features include:

- 100 never-before-seen scrapbook pages
- Tips on recording your family history and scrapbooking with heirlooms
- A new Monogram Alphabet you can create
- A special section showcasing scrapbook products perfect for black-and-white photos and heritage memorabilia

68 pages for $5.95

❹ *Marvelous Scrapbook Makeovers*

Have you ever finished a scrapbook page and thought "something just isn't right"? *Creating Keepsakes* can help with our *Marvelous Scrapbook Makeovers* idea book. Give those scrapbook pages a face-lift with coveted tips and techniques from top scrapbook designers around the country. Whether you're a beginner or a seasoned veteran, perk up your pages with:

- 90 never-before-seen pages and makeover examples
- A FREE template

- Articles on focal point, color, shape, artful arrangement and enhancements
- A glossary of terms

86 pages for $4.95

❺ *The 1999 Scrapbook Hall of Fame*

Creating Keepsakes magazine is proud to present the top 25 scrapbookers from around the world who've been inducted into our 1999 Scrapbook Hall of Fame. We've taken a sample of their best work and published it here for you to enjoy. Features include:

- Over 300 never-before-seen scrapbook pages
- 50 incredible honorable-mention layouts
- Tips and tricks from our readers

168 pages for $14.95

❻ *The 2000 Scrapbook Idea Book*

Make your memories last into the millennium with *Creating Keepsakes'* brand-new idea annual—*The 2000 Scrapbook Idea Book*. Turn to the ultimate resource for new layout ideas on everything from candid kids to active teenagers to seasonal snapshots. Find an idea and create your own from it.

- Over 365 never-before-seen scrapbook pages
- A new Groovy Alphabet you can create
- Cut 'n copy page titles and phrases

168 pages for $14.95

FROM THE STORK

❼ *Winter Holidays*

From Thanksgiving to Hanukkah, and from Christmas to Kwanzaa and even New Year's, the *Winter Holidays* special issue from *Creating Keepsakes* will give you plenty of ideas to fill your scrapbook with seasonal cheer. This special issue is sure to be your favorite gift under the tree with:

• 100 cool scrapbook page ideas
• A Below Freezing Alphabet you can create
• Festive cut 'n copy page accents
• Hundreds of holiday products
• Tips for taking perfect holiday pictures

68 pages for $5.95

❽ *Wedding Scrapbooks*

Whether you're backtracking to your wedding day or the wedding is just around the corner, *Creating Keepsakes* can help you create the perfect wedding album. This special issue includes:

• Over 80 layout ideas on everything from getting hitched to honeymooning
• 28 terrific page titles
• An elegant Wedding Alphabet you can create
• Cut 'n copy page accents
• FREE Paper Whispers sticker from Mrs. Grossman's

68 pages for $4.95

❾ *Vacation Idea Book*

Your vacation may last 10 days, but your memories should last forever. So get your getaway pictures out of that dusty box and into a fun memory album with the *Vacation Idea Book*. Whether you've been frolicking in the sun or exploring hidden treasures, you'll love these fantastic features:

• 12 terrific tips to create travel pages
• An Expedition Alphabet you can create
• 70 breathtaking scrapbook page ideas
• FREE stickers from The Gifted Line

36 pages for $6.95

SCRAPBOOK SOFTWARE

❿ *"The Best of Creative Lettering" CD Vol. 1*

Could your handwriting use a little lift? Now you've got hassle-free handwriting right at your fingertips with "The Best of Creative Lettering" CD Vol. 1 from *Creating Keepsakes*. We've collected your favorite fonts and lettering graphics from past issues of *Creating Keepsakes* magazine, and now you can easily install them on your computer. Features include:

• Windows™ and Macintosh™ compatible
• Perfect for scrapbooking and craft projects
• Sample scrapbook page(s) for each font
• An 11" x 14" fold-out, illustrated guide of all fonts and graphics on the CD

• 15 handwritten, TrueType® fonts
• 600+ lettering graphics and phrases

Only $14.95

⓫ *"The Best of Creative Lettering" CD Vol. 2*

Ready to add even more creative flair to your handwriting? Get 15 all-new fonts and hundreds of lettering graphics with "The Best of Creative Lettering" CD Vol. 2 from *Creating Keepsakes*. This CD contains all the features from Vol. 1 plus:

• Screen saver slide show with sample scrapbook pages
• NEW! Colorized fonts in a browser that allows you to type words, phrases and sentences and paste them into other applications

Only $14.95

Order your new ideas today!

**Call
1-888-247-5282**

**Click
www.creatingkeepsakes.com**

QXXAA

Seize the Moment

Enjoy life's simple joys

WHEN MY OLDEST SON TURNED nine, I suffered an unexpected panic attack. Suddenly I realized that Kade was halfway to adulthood. "Only nine more years to teach him everything he needs to know to survive on his own," I thought sadly. I sensed the huge void our family would feel when Kade left home, and I wished I could somehow slow time down.

I remember experiencing a similar panic attack when Kade was a newborn. I thought, "I'm never going to have a normal night's sleep again—this little guy's going to be attached to me forever." I wished I could speed time up a little. How different one's perspective is looking backward rather than forward.

A great philosopher once said, "Life is but a series of moments. Start living those moments and the years will take care of themselves." The older I get, the more I realize that true happiness can only happen on a moment-to-moment basis. The seemingly insignificant moments often become our happiest memories.

Just three short years ago, an announcement appeared in *Creating Keepsakes* about the birth of my daughter (left). Now, 36 months later, I look at the photo of me and Brecken (below) and sincerely don't know where the time's gone. Thankfully I was able to relax more with my third child and enjoy the wonders of having a new baby. Don't ever take the precious moments with your baby for granted.

A co-worker recently shared a story that reinforced my feelings. She said, "After years of infertility tests, my sister and her husband decided to adopt a baby from Korea. In October 1999, they learned that a beautiful baby girl was available. They quickly filled out the stacks of paperwork and waited to get clearance from the government.

"As each day passed, the wait became increasingly unbearable. I wondered about the baby's progress. Was she sitting up, smiling, laughing? Was she loved and being taken care of? In early November, my sister learned that Bailey—the little girl—had undergone a hernia operation. My sister was sick that she couldn't be there to help take care of Bailey.

"As I watched my sister's frustration, I thought of all the 'firsts' Bailey was experiencing without her mom and dad. Suddenly I realized how important every small moment is—from seeing the baby smile to rocking the baby to sleep. When Bailey finally arrived home in December 1999, it was a joy to see her parents savoring every moment of her life!" ♥

Lisa Bearnson

Record the memories of life's simple moments in your scrapbook.
Supplies *Mulberry paper:* PrintWorks; *Raffia:* Paper Adventures; *Baby announcement:* Designed by Brian Tippetts.

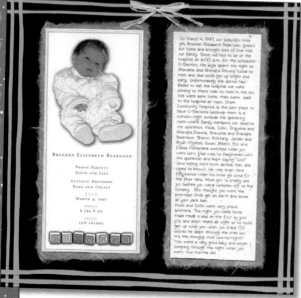

Paper edge: Heartstrings by Fiskars; Photo of Lisa and Brecken by Becky Higgins

From birth announcements to birthday parties, from family vacations to graduation day, D.O.T.S.® rubber-stamp designs and exclusive Close to My Heart™ products will help you to preserve each stage of your baby's life . . . beautifully. With over 64 matching colors of Exclusive Inks and Background and Texture Papers to choose from, your projects will become treasures that will leave a lasting legacy for generations to come. Whether you're interested in purchasing D.O.T.S.® products, hosting a home demonstration, or learning more about the D.O.T.S.® business opportunity, call us today!

D.O.T.S.
DOZENS OF TERRIFIC STAMPS®

1-888-655-6552
www.dotadventures.com

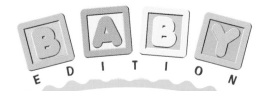

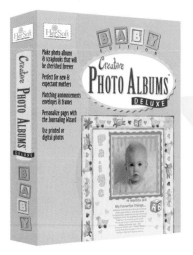

LOOKIN' GOOD

Parker Jensen
6 months old

January 1999

"Parker Jensen"
by Jennifer Jensen
Hurricane, Utah
SUPPLIES
Patterned paper: Paper Pizazz, Hot Off The Press
Wood-frame stationery: Frances Meyer
Computer font: DJ Classic, Fontastic!, D.J. Inkers

"Kenneth"

by Brenda Bennett
Morenci, Arizona

S U P P L I E S

Patterned paper: Over The Moon Press

Colored pencils: Prismacolor, Sanford

Pen: Hybrid Gel Roller, Pentel

Computer font: Bradley Hand, Microsoft Word

Rubber stamps: Stampin' Up!

Embossing powder: Comotion Rubber Stamps

Photo corners: Pebbles in my Pocket

"God Blessed Us America"

by Cynthia Castelluccio
Carrollton, Virginia

S U P P L I E S

Patterned paper: Creative Memories

Corrugated die cuts: DMD Industries

Pens: Le Plume II, Marvy Uchida;
Zig Writer, EK Success; Milky Gel Roller, Pentel

Flag: Cynthia's own design

"Baby Jack"

by Karen Towery
Dallas, Georgia

S U P P L I E S

Specialty paper: The Lacey Paper Company (mulberry paper)

Corner slot punch: Double Scallop, Family Treasures

Computer font: Gigi, Microsoft Word

Wasn't my big brother cute? He was only 18 months old in this picture.

"Spencer"
by Brittany Boice
Mom and Me Scrapbooking
Salt Lake City, Utah
SUPPLIES
Paper-doll die cut: Stamping Station
Pen: Zig Writer, EK Success
Hole punches: Punchline, McGill
Patterned paper: Keeping Memories Alive
Scissors: Dragonback edge, Fiskars
Tug boats: Brittany's own designs

Look who just turned one! Scott Lee Mitchell, my younger brother, had this photo taken for the local newspaper on his first birthday. Mom says that on the very day of this photo, Scotty started walking! He wasn't really talking much—mostly due to the fact that he didn't need to—his older twin siblings, Brice & I, did all the talking for him! Mom was constantly plagued with, "Mommy, Scotty wants a drink," or "Scotty wants a cracker." Grandma Lee made this cute jumper for Scotty for Christmas. This photo really captures Scotty's personality—sparkling & fun!

JANUARY 2, 1978

Snips 'n snails & puppy dog tails... that's what little boys are made of!

"Scotty"
by Brenda Bennett
Morenci, Arizona
SUPPLIES
Patterned paper: Close To My Heart/D.O.T.S.
Lettering template: Classic, Pebble Tracers, Pebbles in my Pocket
Pen: Zig Writer, EK Success
Photo corners: Canson
Idea to note: Brenda got the idea for the dog from Scotty's jumper.

"Harrison Oliver James"
by Ellen James
Orem, Utah
SUPPLIES
Patterned paper: Close To My Heart/D.O.T.S.
Letter die cuts: Ellison
Pen: Zig Opaque Writer, EK Success

Paper edge: Corkscrew by Fiskars

"Chelsea"

by Brenda Bennett
Morenci, Arizona
SUPPLIES

Patterned paper: Close To My Heart/D.O.T.S.

Rubber stamps: D.O.T.S.

Embossing powder: D.O.T.S.

Colored pencils: Prismacolor, Sanford

Pen: Hybrid Gel Roller, Pentel

Photo corners: Canson

Other: Brenda used Archival Mist to deacidify the baby announcement, then included it on the layout.

Idea to note: Brenda embossed the stamped image with white embossing powder, then daubed an inked sponge over the image.

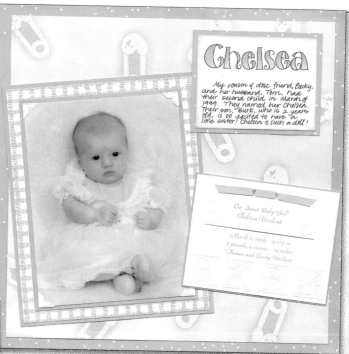

"Cameron's Blessing"

by Nancy Church
Augusta, Georgia
SUPPLIES

Specialty paper: Lasting Impressions (embossed paper)

Computer font: CK Calligraphy, "The Best of Creative Lettering" CD Vol. 1, *Creating Keepsakes*

Embossing template: Lasting Impressions

Ink pad: Splendor, Tsukineko

Idea to note: Nancy placed vellum over the mint-green cardstock, which muted the color.

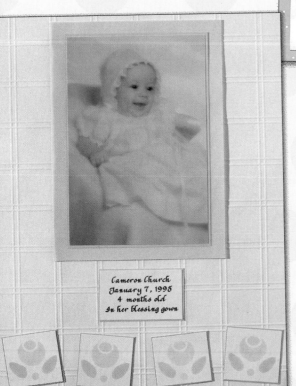

"Double the Blessings"

by Brenda Bennett
Morenci, Arizona
SUPPLIES

Patterned paper: Close To My Heart/D.O.T.S.

Rubber stamps: D.O.T.S.

Embossing powder: D.O.T.S.

Computer font: CK Script, "The Best of Creative Lettering" CD Vol. 1, *Creating Keepsakes*

Pen: Hybrid Gel Roller, Pentel

Chalk: Craf-T Products

Photo corners: Canson

Idea to note: Brenda sponged the edges of the journaling and title with pink ink.

Cheryle Ann

My Mother, Cheryle Ann Lee was born to Earl and Genevieve Lee on June 25, 1951 in Little Hospital in Salt Lake City, Utah. This picture was taken for Mom's first birthday! Grandma Lee made this cute little birthday dress, just as she made most of Mom's clothes. Grandma Lee loves to tell stories of how Mom and her older brother, Rick, would play outside for hours. Rick would come inside and have not a speck of dirt on him, but Mom would come inside covered from head to toe in dirt! Mom was serious about her playtime! What a darling little girl!

UTAH 1952

"Cheryle Ann"
by Brenda Bennett
Morenci, Arizona
SUPPLIES
Patterned paper: Northern Spy
Rubber stamps: D.O.T.S.
Stripe template: D.O.T.S.
Ink pad: Stampin' Up!
Embossing powder: D.O.T.S.
Computer font: CK Script, "The Best of Creative Lettering" CD
Vol. 1, *Creating Keepsakes*
Chalk: Craf-T Products
Photo corners: Pebbles in my Pocket
Idea to note: Brenda used the stripe template, a sponge
and an ink pad to make her own background paper.

"Amber in Her Cute Garanimals"
by Amber Blakesley
Provo, Utah
SUPPLIES
Rainbow and star die cuts: Ellison
Star punch. Marvy Uchida
Pen: Milky Gel Roller, Pentel
Idea to note: Amber repeated the rainbow
pattern in her outfit on the layout.

Nancy
7 Months Old

"Nancy"
by Nancy Church
Augusta, Georgia
SUPPLIES
Specialty paper: Frances Meyer (embossed paper)
Floral stationery card: CR Gibson
Computer font: CK Calligraphy, "The Best of Creative Lettering" CD
Vol. 1, *Creating Keepsakes*

Paper edge: Corkscrew by Fiskars

babies

Rick

I made these finger puppets out of felt for Rick when he was a baby. Now they have gone through all five children. But alas, I am afraid they will not last much longer. I wanted to preserve them somehow, so I recreated them out of paper for this page. These are the first pictures taken of the children (after newborn). Rick and Anna are almost 5 months, Abby is 7, Rex is 5 and Emmy is 9 months old.

Abby

Rex

Anna

Emmy

"Babies"

by Angelyn Bryce
West Chester, Pennsylvania

SUPPLIES

Lettering template: Hand Drawn, Pebble Tracers, Pebbles in my Pocket

Alphabet letters: Alphabitties, Repositionable Sticky Die-Cut Letters, Provo Craft

Computer font: DJ Doodlers, Fontastic!, D.J. Inkers

Corner punches (hearts and circles): McGill

Idea to note: When Angelyn's first child was born, she made finger puppets. After being enjoyed by five children, the beloved finger puppets are starting to fall apart. To remember these special toys, Angelyn re-created the puppets using paper for her layout.

Paper edge: Corkscrew by Fiskars; Embossing templates: Lasting Impressions for Paper; Congratulations card by Lasting Impressions for Paper in Bountiful, UT

JOURNALING IDEA:

Is there a favorite song that you sing to your baby? A favorite finger play you do or story you tell? Don't forget to include memories of and words to these special songs, games and stories in your scrapbook.

"Lane"
by Sonya Wilkinson-Wyeth
Lansing, Michigan

SUPPLIES

Lettering template: Classic Caps, Frances Meyer
Border and bow stickers: Frances Meyer
Heart punch: Marvy Uchida
Pen: Zig Writer, EK Success

"I Am a Child of God"
by Lori Bergmann
Turlock, California

SUPPLIES

Stationery: Bo-Bunny Press
Pen: Zig Writer, EK Success

"Keaton"
by Jana Francis
Provo, Utah

SUPPLIES

Patterned paper: Provo Craft
Alphabet letters: Making Memories
Colored pencils: Memory Pencils, EK Success
Butterfly: Jana's own design

"Lil' Rascals"

by Jennifer Jensen
Hurricane, Utah

SUPPLIES

Frames: NRN Designs
Corner punch: Teardrop, Family Treasures
Stickers: Frances Meyer
Computer font: DJ Calli, Fontastic!, D.J. Inkers
Page title: Page Toppers, Cock-A-Doodle Design, Inc.
Ideas to note: Jennifer printed the journaling on brown vellum. She also included a ribbon on the layout.

PHOTO TIP:

Try taking at
least one roll of
black-and-white film
per year. In general,
black-and-white
photos (taken with
true black-and-white
film) last longer
than color photos.

PHOTO TIP:

Because your baby recognizes your voice,
you can coax him or her into looking into
the camera lens or smiling.

Paper edge: Corkscrew by Fiskars; Embossing template: Lasting Impressions for Paper; Bib by Lasting Impressions for Paper in Bountiful, UT

"By the Window"

by Heidi Prince
Cumming, Georgia
SUPPLIES
Egg punch: Family Treasures
Hole punch: Punchline, McGill
Photo corners: Pebbles in my Pocket

Computer font: Scrap Rhapsody, Lettering
Delights Vol. 2, Inspire Graphics
Scissors: Deckle edge, Fiskars
Idea to note: Heidi used the egg punch
to make the rosebuds—she simply
trimmed off the top of the egg.

"Papi and Mommy"

by Alycia Alvarez
Altus, Oklahoma
SUPPLIES
Stationery: Creative Memories
Computer fonts: CK Expedition and CK Script,
"The Best of Creative Lettering" CD Vol. 1,
Creating Keepsakes
Corner punch: Southwest, McGill
Pen: Zig Writer, EK Success

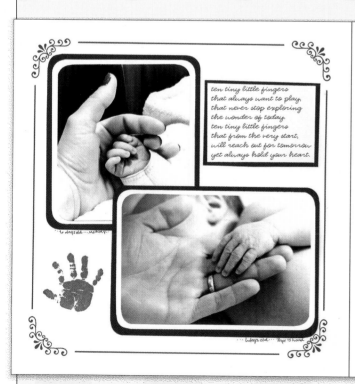

Little Sunday Suit

Aunt Jennifer let Mommy borrow this little tuxedo for
Bobby to wear. He was blessed in it and wore it every
sunday because Mommy loved it.
Spring 1993

Blue-eyed Angel

Heavenly Father sent us a perfect angel,
his eyes are bright and blue.
Bobby's smile shines like heaven's light,
when he looks up at you.
His loving nature warms the soul,
and fills our hearts with joy.
Each day I thank the Lord above,
for our perfect little boy.

"Little Sunday Suit"

by Marilyn Healey
West Jordan, Utah
SUPPLIES

Stationery (suit with stars): Sonburn
Patterned paper: Provo Craft
Computer font: DJ Serif, Dazzle Daze, D.J. Inkers
Star punch: McGill
Poem: by Cynthia M. Anning (modified)
Bow: Marilyn's own design

"Elizabeth Anne Olson"

by Jodi Olson
Redmond, Washington
SUPPLIES

Patterned paper: Colors By Design
Flower die cuts: Pebbles in my Pocket
Punches: Family Treasures (birch leaf, spiral);
Marvy Uchida (circles)
Pen: Zig Millennium, EK Success
Specialty paper: Wintech (Vivelle plush paper)

Elizabeth Anne Olson
1 year old

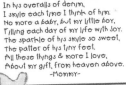

In his overalls of denim,
I smile each time I think of him.
No more a baby, but my little boy,
Filling each day of my life with joy.
The sparkle of his smile so sweet,
The patter of his tiny feet.
All these things & more I love,
About my gift, from heaven above.
—Mommy—

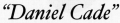

Parker Jensen
1 year old
August 1999

Daniel
Cade

— MAY 1983 —

"Parker Jensen in His Overalls"

by Jennifer Jensen
Hurricane, Utah
S U P P L I E S

Patterned paper: Northern Spy
Pooh Bear die cut: Michel & Company
Computer font: DJ Crayon, Fontastic!, D.J. Inkers
Photo corners: D.O.T.S.

"Daniel Cade"

by Vicki Garner
Windows of Time
Hooper, Utah
S U P P L I E S

Patterned paper: Frances Meyer
Paper-piecing pattern: Baby Theme Pack, Windows of Time
Computer font: Comic Sans MS, Print Artist
Star punch: Marvy Uchida
Pen: Zig Writer, EK Success

Paper edge: Corkscrew by Fiskars

"Little Girls Are Heaven's Flowers"

by Cynthia Castelluccio
Carrollton, Virginia
SUPPLIES

Specialty paper: Frances Meyer (handmade paper);
Wintech (Vivelle plush paper); HyGloss (velour paper);
The Write Stock (vellum paper)
Circle punch: Family Treasures
Pen: Metallic Gel Roller, Marvy Uchida
Flowers: Cynthia's own designs
Idea to note: Cynthia made the bows from raffia.

"Priceless Little Parts"

by Jennifer Jensen
Hurricane, Utah
SUPPLIES

Specialty paper: The Paper Company
(patterned vellum)
Footprint stationery: Creative Papers, CR Gibson
Computer font: DJ Classic, Fontastic!, D.J. Inkers
Poem: From *The Scrapbooker's Best Friend II*,
Chatterbox
Idea to note: Jennifer used ribbon to
make the photo corners.

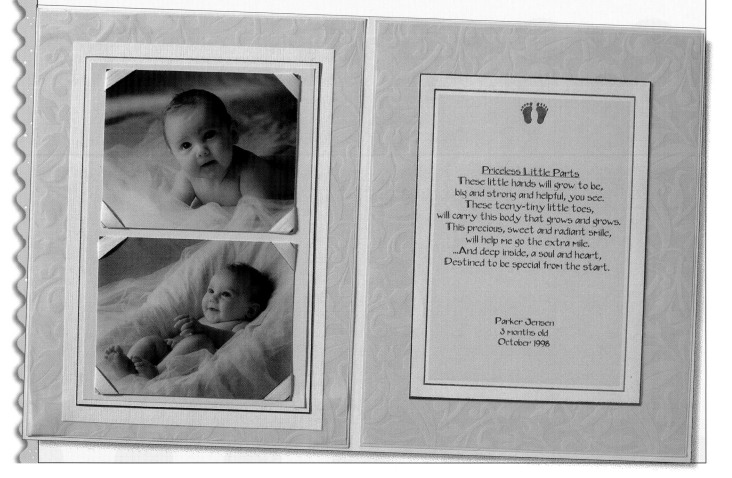

Priceless Little Parts
These little hands will grow to be,
big and strong and helpful, you see.
These teeny-tiny little toes,
will carry this body that grows and grows.
This precious, sweet and radiant smile,
will help me go the extra mile.
...And deep inside, a soul and heart,
Destined to be special from the start.

Parker Jensen
3 months old
October 1998

Tyler likes to sit by the window and watch Teega play in the yard. 9 months 1998

Paper edge: Corkscrew by Fiskars; Embossing template: Lasting Impressions for Paper; Bottle by Lasting Impressions for Paper in Bountiful, UT

PHOTO TIP:

Don't forget to take the three-, four- or five-generation photos. This is an incredible way to connect generations.

"Watching Teega"
by Nancy Church
Augusta, Georgia
SUPPLIES
Patterned paper: Provo Craft
Punches: McGill (small and medium flower); Westrim Crafts (large flower)
Hole punches: Punchline, McGill
Pen: Zig Writer, EK Success

"What Would I Do Without You?"
by Brittany Boice
Mom and Me Scrapbooking
Salt Lake City, Utah
SUPPLIES
Punches: All Night Media (large and small flower, large and small spiral, small sun); Marvy Uchida (large sun, small daisy); Family Treasures (large daisy, leaf); McGill (tulip)
Hole punches: Punchline, McGill
Computer font: Formal Script, Print Artist Platinum, Sierra
Idea to note: Brittany used a small leaf punch to create some of the flowers.

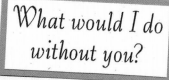

What would I do without you?

This is my mother when she was only a year old. I hope that my children are as beautiful and sweet as she is.

"I Love My Brother" and Sisters

by Kari Hellbusch
American Fork, Utah

S U P P L I E S

Patterned paper: Provo Craft
Computer font: DJ Squared,
Fontastic!, D.J. Inkers

I love my brother and sisters.
Ryanne six weeks old.
September, 1999

"Casey Elizabeth Gabbard"

by Irma Lozano Gabbard
San Diego, California

S U P P L I E S

Patterned paper: GeoPapers
Daisy punch: Family Treasures
Computer font: Freehand, Microsoft Word

Casey Elizabeth Gabbard
November 1992

Rick, born March 26, 91 in Provo, UT., 6
16, 2 oz., 19 inches long.
Anna, born Sept. 2, 92 in Tacoma, WA.,
7 lb. 11 oz., 19 inches long.
Abby, born Sept. 19, 93 in St. George,
UT., 7 lbs., 19 inches long.
Rex, born June 24, 95 in St. George,
UT., 7 lbs. 2 oz., 18 inches long.
Emerald, born Dec. 4, 97 in West
Chester, PA., 8 lbs., 20 inches long.

"Farm Animals"

by Angelyn Bryce
West Chester, Pennsylvania
SUPPLIES

Grass die cuts: Source unknown
Chalk: Craf-T Products
Computer font: DJ Crayon, Fontastic!, D.J. Inkers
Pen: Zig Writer, EK Success
Idea to note: Angelyn got the idea for the animals
and the tree from a piece of fabric.

Memorabilia Idea:

If your baby has a favorite comfort toy, blanket

or pacifier, be sure to include a portion of the item in your scrapbook.

Color copies work well for large items, but pacifiers, for example,

may fit in some of the memorabilia pockets available.

Paper edge: Corkscrew by Fiskars; Rubber stamps: D.O.T.S.; Cards by Sherry Clements of D.O.T.S. in Pleasant Grove, UT

"Parker Jensen, 9 Months Old"

by Jennifer Jensen
Hurricane, Utah
S U P P L I E S
Patterned paper: Over The Moon
Press (plaid); Source unknown
(anchors)

Computer font: DJ Dash,
Fontastic!, D.J. Inkers
Photo corners: D.O.T.S.
Boat: Jennifer's own design
Idea to note: Jennifer used canvas
and string to make the boat.

"Two by Two"

by Brenda Bennett
Morenci, Arizona
S U P P L I E S
Patterned paper: Paperbilities,
MPR (polka dot); Paper Pizazz,
Hot Off The Press (wood)
Ark and animals template:
Noah's Ark, Provo Craft

Chalk: Craf-T Products
Pen: Hybrid Gel Roller, Pentel
Colored pencils: Prismacolor,
Sanford
Computer font: DJ Dash,
Fontastic!, D.J. Inkers
Crocodiles and title lettering:
Brenda's own designs

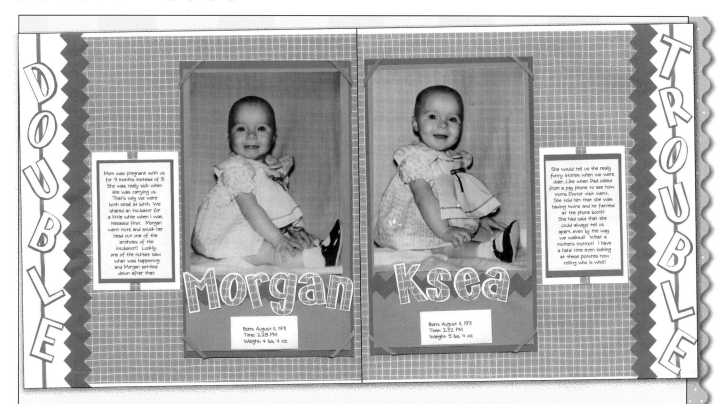

Mom was pregnant with us for 9 months instead of 8. She was really sick when she was carrying us. That's why we were both small at birth. We shared an incubator for a little while when I was released first. Morgan went nuts and stuck her head out one of the armholes of the incubator!! Luckily, one of the nurses saw what was happening and Morgan settled down after that.

She would tell us the really funny stories when we were older...Like when Dad called from a pay phone to see how moms Doctor visit went. She told him that she was having twins and he fainted at the phone booth! She had said that she could always tell us apart...even by the way we walked!! What a mothers instinct! I have a hard time even looking at these pictures now telling who is who!!

Born: August 11, 1971
Time: 2:28 PM
Weight: 4 lbs. 4 oz

Born: August 11, 1971
Time: 2:32 PM
Weight: 5 lbs. 4 oz

"Double Trouble"

by Ksea An Cantonwine
Chehalis, Washington
S U P P L I E S
Patterned paper: Close To My Heart/D.O.T.S.
Lettering template: Classic, Pebble Tracers, Pebbles in my Pocket
Computer font: CK Journaling, "The Best of Creative Lettering" CD Vol. 1, *Creating Keepsakes*
Idea to note: Ksea used ribbon to create a unique effect on the photo corners.

"Thank Heaven for Tanner"

by Marci Leishman
Draper, Utah
S U P P L I E S
Patterned paper: Karen Foster
Computer font: DJ Picket, Inspirations, D.J. Inkers
Pen: Zig Clean Color, EK Success

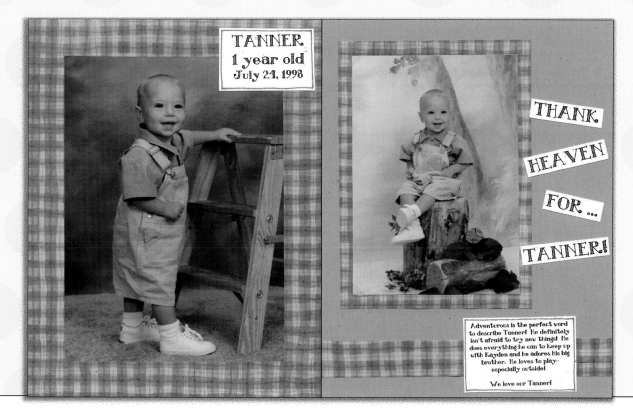

TANNER.
1 year old
July 24, 1998

THANK. HEAVEN FOR. ... TANNER!

Adventurous is the perfect word to describe Tanner! He definitely isn't afraid to try new things! He does everything he can to keep up with Kayden and he adores his big brother. He loves to play—especially outside!

We love our Tanner!

Paper edge: Corkscrew by Fiskars

"Katie's First Year"

by Stephanie Barnard
Laguna Niguel, California

SUPPLIES

Computer font: Source unknown

Pen: Zig Writer, EK Success

Idea to note: What a fun idea to show each month of Katie's first year in a single layout!

Katie's First Year

*Your first year of life is over
Katie our beautiful daughter.
We are so very proud to be
your Mother and Father.*

*It doesn't seem like it's been a year
Since we first held you close.
For all the changes that we made
It's you that changed the most.*

*Your sweet smile, those big eyes
Are but just a few,
Of the many wonderful things
That we love about you.*

*We love your hugs and kisses,
We grab and hold you tight.
Sometimes we peek into your room
To watch you sleep at night.*

*We'll cherish these young years
Because this much we know,
It won't be long before you're grown
And we'll have to let you go.*

Katie, we love you!

"Row, Row, Row Your Boat"

by Alycia Alvarez
Altus, Oklahoma

SUPPLIES

Patterned paper: The Paper Patch

Corner slot punch: Double Scallop, Family Treasures

Pen: Gelly Roll, Sakura

Tie Me To The Moon's Baby Album

Here's a great place to store your baby's scrapbook pages—Tie Me To The Moon's Be Still My Heart baby album. This uniquely crafted, 12" x 12" post-bound album is sure to be the highlight of any nursery. The album even comes with 30 sheets of white-on-white paper. (Don't forget to look for Tie Me To The Moon's coordinating stickers.)

MSRP: $39.95–49.95
Phone: 888/509-2193
(information and wholesale orders)
Web site: . . . .
www.goodstuffhere.com

Check your favorite scrapbook supply store.

*8 Big
Products for Your
Little One*

Moon Prints' Finger Frames and Footsie Frames

Preserve your little one's handprints and footprints with Moon Prints' do-it-yourself picture frame kits. Each kit comes with non-toxic paint and a picture frame. Create your own memorable frame or birth announcement, or include your little one's handprints and footprints in a scrapbook.

MSRP: $4.99–6.99
Phone: 888/689-7919
Web site: . . . . www.moonprints.com

Check your favorite craft or scrapbook supply store.

WhipperSnapper Designs' WhipperClipper Scrapbook Vol. 1 Clip Art

Add fun enhancements to your scrapbook pages or create birth announcements or party favors with WhipperSnapper Designs' WhipperClipper Scrapbook Vol. 1 clip art. This Mac and PC compatible CD contains over 240 graphic images that can easily be adapted to any layout you're working on.

MSRP: $30
Phone: 719/633-8631

Check your favorite scrapbook supply store.

me & my BIG ideas' Patterned Paper and Stickers

Need some great accents to welcome your little one to the world? Check out me & my BIG ideas' adorable baby-themed 12" x 12" patterned paper and coordinating stickers. These items help you make terrific pages in a snap.

Phone: . . . . 949/589-4607 (wholesale only)
Web site: . . . . *www.meandmybigideas.com*

Check your favorite scrapbook supply store.

All My Memories' Album-Cover Patterns

If you're in search of an album that coordinates with your baby's nursery, check out the fun new album-cover patterns from All My Memories. The patterns are easily adapted to both 12" x 12" and 8½" x 11" albums, and can be made with a minimal amount of sewing.

MSRP: $6.99
Phone: . . . . 888/553-1998 (wholesale only)

Check your favorite scrapbook supply store.

Use the Memory Button to record your baby's first words. *Layout by Cindy Tingey of The Paper Attic in Sandy, Utah. Die-cut art by Janet Lee of Stamping Station in Layton, Utah.* **Supplies** *Patterned paper:* Paper Pizzaz, Hot Off The Press; *Die cuts:* Stamping Station; *Scissors:* Mini-Scallop edge, Fiskars; *Punch:* McGill; *Chalk:* Craf-T Products; *Repositionable sticky die cuts:* Alphabitties, Provo Craft; *Computer font:* Scrap Simple, Lettering Delights Vol. 2, Inspire Graphics; *Memory Button:* Memory Technology, Inc.

All My Memories' Pea-Head Calendars and Idea Book

Enjoy your baby all year long with All My Memories' new Pea-Head calendars and idea book. Use the idea book to help you assemble the months on the calendar. Then, simply add photos of your little one and record your baby's milestones throughout the year. At the end of the year, just slip the calendar sheets into your scrapbook. (Calendars are available in both 8½" x 11" and 12" x 12" sizes.)

MSRP: $7.99–11.99
Phone: . . . . 888/553-1998 (wholesale only)

Product Picks

Memory Technology's Memory Button

Instantly recall your baby's first words or funny things he or she says with the Memory Button by Memory Technology, Inc. Simply press the record button and record your baby's voice, include the Memory Button on a layout, then press the play button to play back your baby's words any time you like. (Don't forget to record short personal messages from parents, grandparents and siblings.)

MSRP: $14.99
Phone: 877/636-2888
Web site: . . . . *www.memorybutton.com*

Karen Foster Design's Journaling Tags on the FunFonts CD

If you're in search of a creative way to journal your baby's milestones, look no further! The journaling tags on Karen Foster Design's new FunFonts CD are terrific. The journaling tag clip-art images print in black-and-white (which you can paint like these shown here) as well as color versions—both of which can be printed with or without journaling lines. This CD is packed with hundreds of clip-art images and over 20 new fonts!

MSRP: $24.95
Phone: . . . . 801/451-9779 (wholesale only)
Web site: . . . . *www.funfonts.com*

Check your favorite scrapbook supply store.

Memories to Last a Lifetime

Remember your first Mother's Day? The hand-picked flowers, the homemade gifts, and hoping you'd never forget a single minute? With our Stampin' Memories® line, you'll always remember those special moments. No matter what you're creating,

Stampin' Up!® has the best stamps and accessories to help bring your memories to life. Our 200-page catalog with its hundreds of exclusive images and ideas includes sheet protectors, papers, inks, and binders with washable linen covers that are perfect for stamping. So call our toll-free number, and let us help you enjoy a lifetime of memories.

DAY IN, DAY OUT

Babies are a
Gift From Heaven
♥ some of our favorite pictures of Brynne ♥

JOURNALING IDEA:

Does your baby sleep in a particular position, or does he or she snuggle with a certain toy or person? Don't forget to record any habits that are particular to your baby.

"Babies Are a Gift from Heaven"
by Jennifer McLaughlin
Back Door Friends—The Scrapbooking Company
Whittier, California
SUPPLIES
Patterned paper: Source unknown
Pen: Zig Writer, EK Success
Colored pencils: Prismacolor, Sanford
Idea to note: Jennifer hung pictures on the layout with wired ribbon.

A baby is
a sweet
new blossom
of humanity
fresh fallen
from God's
own home
to flower
on earth.
Andrew
·1996·

"A Sweet New Blossom of Humanity"
by Alycia Alvarez
Altus, Oklahoma

SUPPLIES

Flower template: Pebble Tracers, Pebbles in my Pocket

Scissors: Seagull edge, Fiskars

Corner slot punch: Family Treasures

Colored pencils: Memory Pencils, EK Success

"This Little Piggie"
by Jodi Olson
Redmond, Washington

SUPPLIES

Patterned paper: Keeping Memories Alive

Punches: Family Treasures (jumbo circle, rectangle); Marvy Uchida (small, medium and large circle, small daisy); All Night Media (mini-spiral)

Hole punch: Punchline, McGill

Pen: Zig Millennium, EK Success

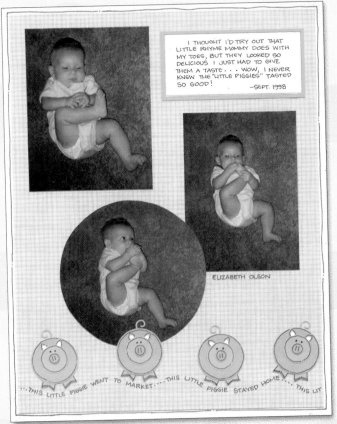

I THOUGHT I'D TRY OUT THAT LITTLE RHYME MOMMY DOES WITH MY TOES, BUT THEY LOOKED SO DELICIOUS I JUST HAD TO GIVE THEM A TASTE . . . WOW, I NEVER KNEW THE "LITTLE PIGGIES" TASTED SO GOOD!
—SEPT. 1998

ELIZABETH OLSON

...THIS LITTLE PIGGIE WENT TO MARKET... THIS LITTLE PIGGIE STAYED HOME... THIS LIT

"Oh Baby! What a Belly Button!"
by Karen Glenn
Orem, Utah

S U P P L I E S

Specialty paper: Frances Meyer
(embossed vellum)
Pen: Zig Writer, EK Success
Colored pencils: Prismacolor, Sanford
Photos: by Ron Morgan

"Megan"
by Denise Stott
Mom and Me Scrapbooking
Salt Lake City, Utah

S U P P L I E S

Patterned paper: Keeping Memories Alive
Punches: Family Treasures (tulip, heart,
medium star); McGill (hand, small star)
Die cuts: Accu-Cut Systems (buttons,
xylophone); Ellison (crayons, letters)
Letter and number template:
Dot Letters, Frances Meyer
Computer font: Scrap Simple, Lettering
Delights Vol. 2, Inspire Graphics

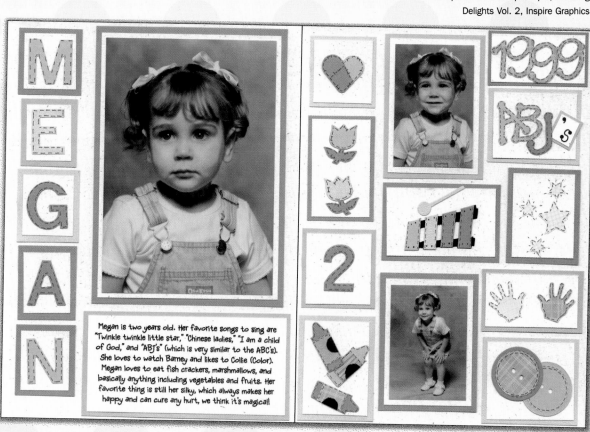

Megan is two years old. Her favorite songs to sing are "Twinkle twinkle little star," "Chinese ladies," "I am a child of God," and "ABJ's" (which is very similar to the ABC's). She loves to watch Barney and likes to Collie (Color). Megan loves to eat fish crackers, marshmallows, and basically anything including vegetables and fruits. Her favorite thing is still her silky, which always makes her happy and can cure any hurt, we think it's magical!

Please Don't Eat the Daisies !

Seventeen months old and teething like crazy! Sarah was delighted to chew on some plastic daisies. It's no coincidence that those flowers matched her new outfit - Mama had pictures to snap! Guess Sarah thought the daisies needed watering, just look at that drool!

Sarah Grace Garrod
January 27, 1999
17 months

"Please Don't Eat the Daisies!"

by Sally Garrod
East Lansing, Michigan
SUPPLIES
Scissors: Clouds and Scallop edges, Fiskars
Punches: Family Treasures (flowers, elegant hearts, tears)
Hole punches: Punchline, McGill
Computer font: DJ Jenn Penn, Fontastic! 2, D.J. Inkers
Idea to note: Sally got the idea for the border from her daughter's dress.

"Zachary"

by Rhonda Solomon
Chandler, Arizona
SUPPLIES
Pen: Zig Writer, EK Success
Chalk: Craf-T Products
Idea to note: Rhonda used twine and clothespins to "hang" her photos on the layout.

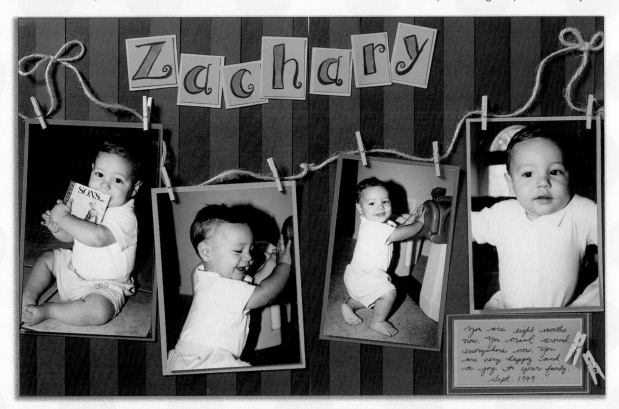

You are eight months now. You crawl around everywhere now. You are very happy and a joy to your family. Sept. 1999

"Little Eyes, Little Nose"

by Rhonda Solomon
Chandler, Arizona
SUPPLIES

Patterned paper: Colors By Design
Scissors: Wave edge, Paper Adventures
Pen: Zig Calligraphy, EK Success

"Enjoying the Flowers"

by Tracy Managan
Pittsburg, California
SUPPLIES

Stationery: MM's Design
Daisy punch: Family Treasures

Hole punch: Punchline, McGill
Pen: Milky Gel Roller, Pentel
Daisies and ladybug: Tracy's
own designs

16 mo.   aug 1999

P
U
S
S
Y
W
I
L
L
O
W

Miriam Elizabeth Morgan

Such a slender, fuzzy-headed darling ~ we call her little ...

"Miriam Elizabeth Morgan"

by Kimberly Ann Morgan
Pleasant Grove, Utah
SUPPLIES
Patterned paper: Memory Press, Downs Printing

Pens: Callipen and Micron Pigma, Sakura
Colored pencils: Prismacolor, Sanford
Pussy willows: Kimberly's own designs

"Sweet Little Daisy"

by Erin Terrell
San Antonio, Texas
SUPPLIES
Patterned paper: Paper Pizazz, Hot Off The Press (purple); Keeping Memories Alive (pink speckled)

Punches: Family Treasures
Hole punches: Punchline, McGill
Eyes: Provo Craft
Pens: Liquid Gold, Marvy Uchida; Zig Writer, EK Success
Angel: Erin's own designs

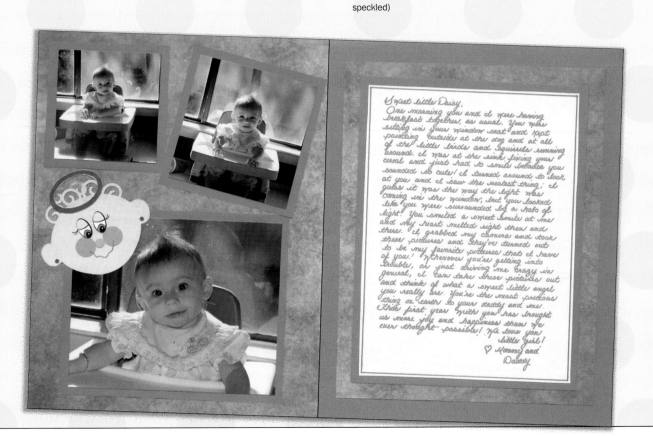

A Wee Bit Of Heaven

our angel...Juliette...

nothing's so sweet as sisters...

December 1994

Some bunny loves me!

"A Wee Bit of Heaven"

by Sharon Lewis
Memory Lane
Mesa, Arizona
SUPPLIES

Patterned paper: Northern Spy
Specialty paper: Paper Adventures (printed vellum)
Scissors: Jumbo Scallop edge, All Night Media
Hole punch: Punchline, McGill
Pen: Micron Pigma, Sakura
Colored pencils: Memory Pencils, EK Success
Lettering idea: "Concave" from *The Art of Creative Lettering* by Creating Keepsakes Books
Ink pad: Stampin' Up!
Photo corners: Boston Int'l
Flowers: Sharon's own designs
Ideas to note: Sharon "tied" on the title with embroidery floss, then used ink from the ink pad to shade the title.

"Some Bunny Loves Me"

by Heidi Prince
Cumming, Georgia
SUPPLIES

Patterned paper:
Paperbilities, MPR
Punches: Family Treasures

Die cuts (ballet shoes and egg): Pebbles in my Pocket
Pen: Evans Craft
Computer font: CK Anything Goes, "The Best of Creative Lettering" CD Vol. 1, *Creating Keepsakes*

Paper edge: Corkscrew by Fiskars

"Jesse Dakota"

by Debi Adams
Anaheim, California
SUPPLIES

Patterned paper: Close To My Heart/D.O.T.S.
(plaid, polka dot); Provo Craft (cow);
Paperbilities, MPR (dark brown)
Decorated die cut: Cross My Heart
Rubber stamps and ink pad: D.O.T.S.
Pen: My Legacy Writer, D.O.T.S.
Colored pencils: Memory Pencils, EK Success
Cactus: Debi's own design
Journaling idea: Debi included the story
of Jesse's adoption on the layout.

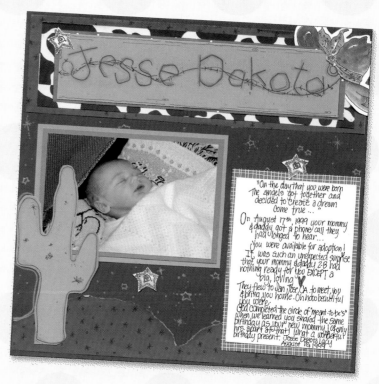

"Denim Dreams"

by Rhonda Solomon
Chandler, Arizona
SUPPLIES

Specialty paper: Paper
Adventures (velveteen paper)
Colored pencils: Memory
Pencils, EK Success

Ideas to note: Rhonda used her
sewing machine to stitch
around the edges of the layout
and embroider the title on velveteen paper. She also included
fabric and yarn from her son's
quilt on the layout.

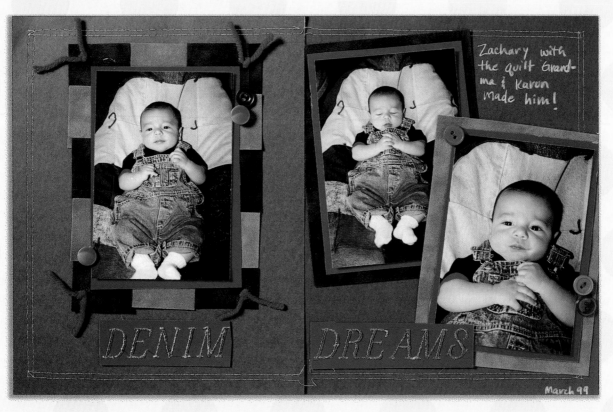

unbearably cute

Daisy (age 13 months) and her teddy bear sitting in Daddy's chair.

Daisy looked adorable in these PJ's! MiMi and Pop Pop gave them to her for her first birthday. The cute Cat-in-the-Hat slippers were from Jason, Jenny and Cole.

Busy Little Bee! At ten months old, Skyler is very curious and in to everything! She keeps mom hopping!

"Unbearably Cute"
by Erin Terrell
San Antonio, Texas
S U P P L I E S
Punches: Marvy Uchida (heart);
Family Treasures (circle)
Bear template: Provo Craft
Pens: Zig Writer, EK Success; Artist, Marvy Uchida
Lettering template: Block Serif,
Pebble Tracers, Pebbles in my Pocket
Idea to note: Erin included fabric and ribbon
from her daughter's pajamas on the layout.

"Busy Little Bee!"
by Shannon Lowe
Salt Lake City, Utah
S U P P L I E S
Patterned paper: Provo Craft
Border stickers (bees): Provo Craft
Computer font: DJ Doodlers, Fontastic!, D.J. Inkers

Paper edge: Corkscrew by Fiskars

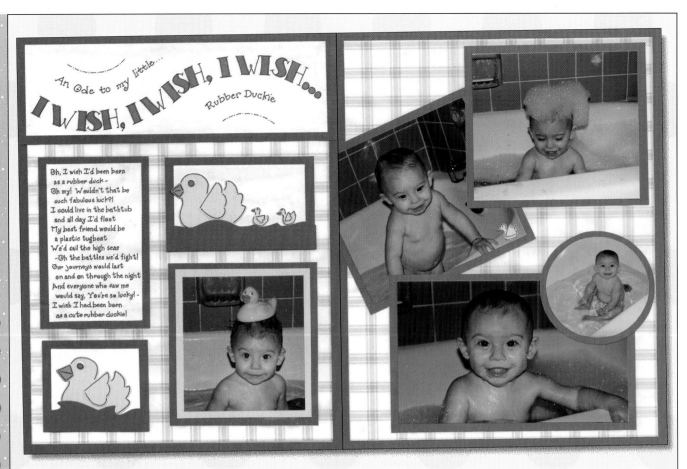

An Ode to my little...

I WISH, I WISH, I WISH...

Rubber Duckie

Oh, I wish I'd been born
as a rubber duck -
Oh my! Wouldn't that be
such fabulous luck?!
I could live in the bathtub
and all day I'd float
My best friend would be
a plastic tugboat
We'd sail the high seas
-Oh the battles we'd fight!
Our journeys would last
on and on through the night
And everyone who saw me
would say, You're so lucky! -
I wish I had been born
as a cute rubber duckie!

"I Wish, I Wish, I Wish"
by Erin Terrell
San Antonio, Texas
SUPPLIES
Patterned paper: The Paper Patch
Duck template: Pebble Tracers, Pebbles in my Pocket
Pen: Zig Writer, EK Success
Computer fonts: DJ FiddleSticks, FiddleSticks, D.J. Inkers;
CK Fill In, "The Best of Creative Lettering" CD Vol. 1,
Creating Keepsakes
Idea to note: Erin placed vellum over the patterned
paper to soften the pattern.

"Tubby Time in Japan"
by Desirée Tanner
Provo Craft
Provo, Utah
SUPPLIES
Patterned paper: Provo Craft
Lettering template: Scrapbook, Provo Craft
Alphabet letters: Alphabitties, Repositionable Sticky
Die-Cut Letters, Provo Craft
Pen: Zig Writer, EK Success
Turtles: Desirée's own designs

SEPTEMBER 10, 1999
19 MONTHS OLD

"Here... have some bubbles!"

McKenna loves Grandma's big tub! I was tending McKenna while I was visiting, and I thought it would be fun for McKenna to play in Grandma's huge tub—and boy was it! She loved it! She was begging Mama I to turn on the water again, but soon she fell in love with the bubbles! She put them all over herself—on her head, her nose, her mouth—everywhere! Then she thought Grandma & Aunt Brenna needed some bubbles too! It's a good thing she's so darn cute!

CLINTON, UTAH

Rub·a·Dub
Kids in a Tub

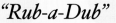

Paper edge: Corkscrew by Fiskars; Die cut: Stamping Station; Die-cut art by Stamping Station in Layton, UT

"Bubble Trouble"

by Brenda Bennett
Morenci, Arizona

SUPPLIES

Patterned paper: Memory Press, Downs Printing
Punches: Family Treasures (large and medium circles); Marvy Uchida (small circle)
Pen: Zig Writer, EK Success
Colored pencils: Prismacolor, Sanford
Specialty paper: The Paper Company (vellum paper)

Ink pads: D.O.T.S.
Tool technique: Brenda ran a sheet of vellum through her Xyron machine, then sponged blue, yellow and pink ink over the vellum. She punched out the circles and sponged the circle edges with a darker shade of ink. Finally she peeled off the adhesive backing and adhered the circles to the layout.

"Rub-a-Dub"

by Jana Francis
Provo, Utah

SUPPLIES

Patterned paper: The Paper Patch
Pen: Zig Calligraphy, EK Success
Tub: Jana's own design

Memorabilia Idea:

Don't forget to include your baby's handprints and footprints in your scrapbook. You may want to do this every six months until your baby is two, then once a year thereafter. These sweet reminders will help mark your child's growth.

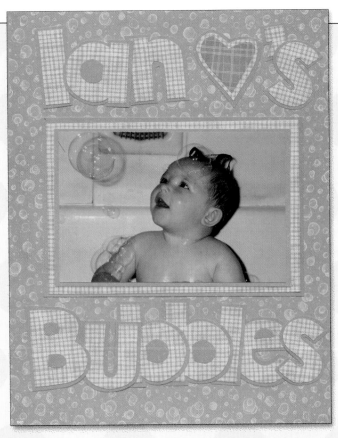

"Footprints and Handprints"

by Kimberly Isaacson
Provo, Utah

SUPPLIES

Patterned paper: Provo Craft (dots); Frances Meyer (gingham, handprints)
Stickers: Frances Meyer
Computer font: DJ Doodlers, Fontastic!, D.J. Inkers
Ink pad: Colorbox, Clearsnap, Inc.

"Ian Loves Bubbles"

by Shannon Wolz
Salt Lake City, Utah

SUPPLIES

Patterned paper: The Paper Patch
Lettering template: Block, Pebble Tracers, Pebbles in my Pocket

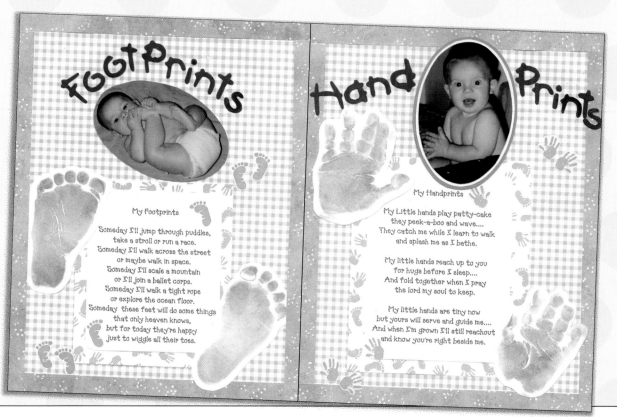

My Footprints

Someday I'll jump through puddles,
take a stroll or run a race.
Someday I'll walk across the street
or maybe walk in space.
Someday I'll scale a mountain
or I'll join a ballet corps.
Someday I'll walk a tight rope
or explore the ocean floor.
Someday these feet will do some things
that only heaven knows,
but for today they're happy
just to wiggle all their toes.

My Handprints

My little hands play patty-cake
they peek-a-boo and wave....
They catch me while I learn to walk
and splash me as I bathe.

My little hands reach up to you
for hugs before I sleep....
And fold together when I pray
the lord my soul to keep.

My little hands are tiny now
but yours will serve and guide me....
And when I'm grown I'll still reachout
and know you're right beside me.

JOURNALING IDEA:

*Make a "My First Home"
layout for your baby's scrapbook
with photos of the exterior of your
home and the baby's nursery.
Be sure to include the address
and phone number on the
layout along with a floor
plan of the house.*

PHOTO TIP:

Capture some of those "silly" moments
of everyday life on film.
Here are some fun reminders:

- Blowing kisses or waving "bye-bye"
- Making funny faces
- Dressing up (or wearing Mom's or Dad's shoes)
- Wearing sunglasses
- Dancing
- Throwing tantrums
- Mischievous moments
- Kissing (friends, siblings or other family members)
- Playing in rain, snow or puddles
- Smelling flowers
- Petting animals at a petting zoo
- Bathing (don't forget to strategically place the washcloth or rubber duck!)
- Potty training
- Naptime
- Outings
- Chicken pox

Tyler had so much fun playing in the snow in her new winter coat! January 1999 Provo, Utah

"Playing in the Snow"
by Nancy Church
Augusta, Georgia
SUPPLIES
Patterned paper: Provo Craft
Specialty paper: NRN Designs (embossed paper)
Rub-on transfers (snowflakes): Provo Craft
Computer font: Scrap Casual, Lettering Delights, Inspire Graphics
Photo corners: Canson

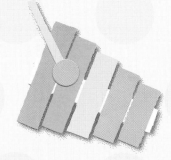

The typical NIGHT NIGHT routine of a two year old:

Step Two: Brusha-Brusha-Brusha! Time to practice good dental hygiene! Daisy prefers to use this time to practice her silly faces in the mirror. She would also rather lick the toothpaste than actually brush her teeth.

Step One: Put on your PJs! Daisy can get the pants all by herself, but daddy has to help with the shirt. These little footed PJ's look really cute on her. She's a doll baby!

Step Three: Read a book! This is Daisy's favorite part of the night. She loves to read and look at books. Her favorite books are ones that teach animals and shapes. She knows all of her basic shapes now: circle, square, rectangle, triangle, moon, star, heart, and oval. She can name most of the animals and do their sounds. She is funniest when she makes the monkey sounds! She likes to read her 'Baby's First Bible' that Zachary gave her. She also loves to read 'Pooh's Five Little Honeypots' and 'The Wheels on the Bus' (the song by the same name also being one of her favorite songs!). Every time we finish reading a book, she'll pull another one off the shelf and say, "Read a book!".

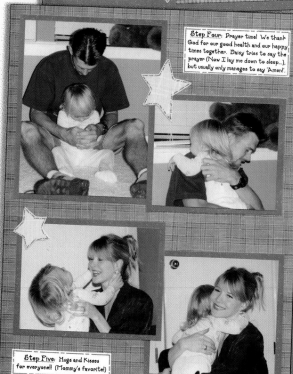

Step Four: Prayer time! We thank God for our good health and our happy times together. Daisy tries to say the prayer (Now I lay me down to sleep...), but usually only manages to say 'Amen!'.

Zzzz...

Step Six: Lie down and *pretend* to go to sleep! Look at that big ol' grin on Daisy's face! She's nowhere near ready for bedtime. She goes to bed at 9:30 every night and usually stays up until about 10:30 or 11:00. She stays in her room and plays quietly, usually looking at books and playing pretend with her stuffed animals. Sometimes she will sneak out of the room and try to see what Mommy and Daddy are up to. We catch her and send her scooting back to bed, after more night-night kisses, of course! She's in her 'big-girl' bed now, meaning that we lowered her crib and took one side off of it so she can come and go as she pleases. This works well because she can come and get us if she needs to go potty during the night. It's also great fun on Saturday mornings to have her come climb into bed with us (bringing all of her stuffed animals with her, usually!) and watch cartoons. The one thing that Daisy cannot sleep without is her dolphin from Sea World that Auntie Angela bought for her. (That little gray thing under her arm in the picture below-'dolphi', as Daisy calls him.)

Step Five: Hugs and kisses for everyone!! (Mommy's favorite!)

"Night-Night Routine"

by Erin Terrell

San Antonio, Texas

SUPPLIES

Patterned paper: Keeping Memories Alive

Alphabet letters: Alphabitties and Funky, Repositionable Sticky Die-Cut Letters, Provo Craft

Die cuts: Stamping Station

Pens: Zig Writer, EK Success

Colored pencils: Prismacolor, Sanford

Computer font: DJ FiddleSticks, FiddleSticks, D.J. Inkers

Paper edge: Corkscrew by Fiskars; Die cut: Pebbles in my Pocket; Die-cut art by Kristy Banks of Highland, UT

"Me and My Dad"
by Kerri Bradford
Orem, Utah
SUPPLIES

Lettering template: Block, Pebble Tracers, Pebbles in my Pocket

Patterned paper: Paperbilities, MPR (checked); Source unknown (bear)

Computer font: Impress True Type, Source unknown

Heart punch: McGill

Bear and heart: Kerri's own designs

"Best Buddies"
by Emily Waters
Provo Craft
Provo, Utah
SUPPLIES

Patterned paper: PrintWorks (striped); Provo Craft (plaid)

Circle punch: Marvy Uchida

Lettering template: Kids, Provo Craft

Computer font: Scrap Simple,
Lettering Delights Vol 2, Inspire Graphics

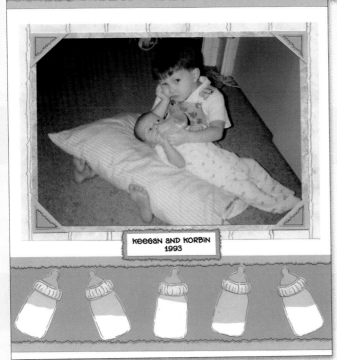

"So This Is What 'Big Brother' Means!"
by Brenée Williams
Boise, Idaho
SUPPLIES

Patterned paper: Provo Craft

Scissors: Deckle edge, Fiskars

Computer font: Comic Sans MS,
Print Artist

Bottles: Baby Bottle,
Provo Craft Micro Template

Specialty paper: CTI Paper USA,
Inc. (vellum paper)

Colored pencils:
Prismacolor, Sanford

Pen: Zig Millennium, EK Success

"Khala"

by Cheryl Souter
Scrapbooker's Paradise
Calgary, Alberta, Canada
SUPPLIES

Patterned paper: Keeping Memories Alive
Specialty paper: Wintech (Vivelle sponge paper)
Heart punch: McGill
Heart die cut: Ellison
Lettering template: Fat Caps, Frances Meyer
Puzzle template: Déjà Views,
The C-Thru Ruler Co.

"Grammy"

by Erin Terrell
San Antonio, Texas
SUPPLIES

Lettering template: Scrapbook, Provo Craft
Sticker: Suzy's Zoo
Pen: Zig Writer, EK Success
Computer font: DJ FiddleSticks, FiddleSticks,
D.J. Inkers

Daisy loves when she gets to spend time with her Grammy. Her eyes just light up when she sees her and she puts her arms out so Grammy will give her a big hug!

I LOVE GRAMMY

Grammy is always fun to hang out with! She takes Daisy sailing out on her boat and lets Daisy swim in the spa in her backyard. Daisy's favorite thing to do at Grammy's house is to chase 'Little Bit', the kitty cat.

Grammy thinks its funny to feed lemons to Daisy and then watch the silly faces that she makes.

"Lil' Lady"
by Brenda Bennett
Morenci, Arizona
SUPPLIES
Patterned paper: Provo Craft
Pen: Zig Writer, EK Success
Title and rope: Brenda's own designs

"Good Morning"
by Emily Magleby
Springville, Utah
SUPPLIES
Patterned paper: The Paper Patch
Punches: Family Treasures (teardrop, leaves);
Marvy Uchida (small, medium and large circle, bow)
Hole punch: Punchline, McGill
Crib die cut: Pebbles in my Pocket
Lettering template: Block, Pebble Tracers,
Pebbles in my Pocket

"Turning 2"
by Karen Glenn
Orem, Utah
SUPPLIES
Patterned paper: NRN Designs
Hole punch: Punchline, McGill
Pen: Zig Clean Color, EK Success
Colored pencils: Prismacolor, Sanford

"Pickin' Flowers"
by Brenda Bennett
Morenci, Arizona
SUPPLIES
Punches: Family Treasures
(large and small daisy, large and small circle,
large flower); Marvy Uchida (small flower);
All Night Media (spiral)
Pens: Zig Writers, EK Success
Colored pencils: Prismacolor, Sanford
Lettering idea: "Flower Garden" from
The Art of Creative Lettering by
Creating Keepsakes Books

Paper edge: Corkscrew by Fiskars

"McKenna"
by Brenda Bennett
Morenci, Arizona
S U P P L I E S
Patterned paper: Frances Meyer
Scissors: Mini-Pinking edge, Fiskars
Punches: Family Treasures
Hole punch: Punchline, McGill
Pen: Zig Writer, EK Success
Colored pencils: Prismacolor, Sanford
Lettering template: Block Serif, Pebble
Tracers, Pebbles in my Pocket
Idea to note: Brenda used circle and
hole punches to make the fruit.

"Cute As a Button"
by Heather Holdaway Thatcher
Draper, Utah
S U P P L I E S
Patterned paper: Frances Meyer
Pens: Zig Writers, EK Success; The Ultimate
Gel Pen, American Craft
Watercolor pencils: Resign
Idea to note: Heather used string
throughout the layout.

"Jayme's First Snowman"
by Amber Blakesley
Provo, Utah
SUPPLIES

Patterned paper: Carolee's Creations
Specialty paper: The Paper Company (vellum paper)
Lettering template: Block Serif,
Pebble Tracers, Pebbles in my Pocket
Idea to note: Amber tore the vellum
to look like snow.

"Peek-a-Boo"
by Sonya Wilkinson-Wyeth
Lansing, Michigan
SUPPLIES

Patterned paper: Northern Spy
Star punches: Marvy Uchida (large);
All Night Media (small)
Lettering template: Block, Pebble Tracers,
Pebbles in my Pocket
Bow stickers: Frances Meyer
Pen: Milky Gel Roller, Pentel

Mmmm... Cheerios, My Favorite!

when I was little, I used to love cheerios! I loved them so much, I took the whole box into the living room and started eating them. (Not to mention the huge mess I made.) But later I had to pick every single one up!

"Mmmm... Cheerios, My Favorite!"
by Sara Talluto
Rochester Hills, Michigan
SUPPLIES
Punches: All Night Media (spiral, small flower);
Marvy Uchida (sun, circle)
Hole punches: Punchline, McGill
Patterned paper: The Paper Patch
Computer font: Source unknown
Pens: Zig Writers, EK Success
Strawberries and bowl: Sara's own designs

ian,

how does your garden grow?

"Ian, How Does Your Garden Grow?"
by Shannon Wolz
Salt Lake City, Utah
SUPPLIES
Patterned paper: Keeping Memories Alive
Stickers: PrintWorks
Pen: Zig Writer, EK Success

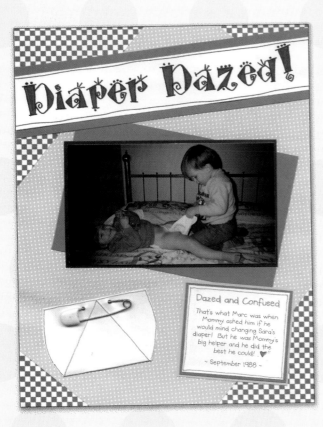

Diaper Dazed!

Dazed and Confused
That's what Marc was when Mommy asked him if he would mind changing Sara's diaper! But he was Mommy's big helper and he did the best he could! ♥
~ September 1988 ~

"Diaper Dazed"
by Pam Talluto
Rochester Hills, Michigan
SUPPLIES
Patterned paper: The Paper Patch
Computer fonts: CK Expedition and CK Toggle,
"The Best of Creative Lettering" CD Vol. 1 and Vol. 2,
Creating Keepsakes
Pens: Zig Writers, EK Success

Paper edge: Corkscrew by Fiskars

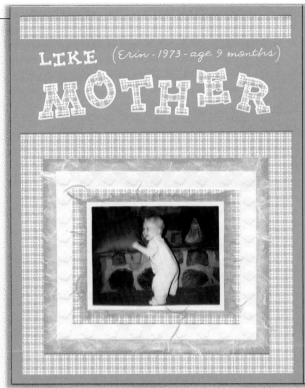

LIKE *(Erin - 1973 - age 9 months)*

MOTHER

LIKE *(Daisy - 1998 - age 10 months)*

DAUGHTER

"Like Mother, Like Daughter"

by Erin Terrell
San Antonio, Texas
SUPPLIES
Patterned paper: Paper
Adventures
Alphabet letters: Alphabitties,
Repositionable Sticky Die-Cut
Letters, Provo Craft

Pen: Milky Gel Roller, Pentel
Lettering template: Scrapbook,
Provo Craft
Specialty paper: Artists Choice
(mulberry paper)
Embossing template:
Provo Craft

"Sunday Stroll"

by Beth Wakulsky
Haslett, Michigan
SUPPLIES
Patterned paper: Paper
Adventures
Alphabet letters: Fat Dot,
Repositionable Sticky Die-Cut
Letters, Provo Craft

Computer font: DJ Doodlers,
Fontastic!, D.J. Inkers
Stroller die cuts: Beth got the
idea from a ScrapEase die cut
by What's New.

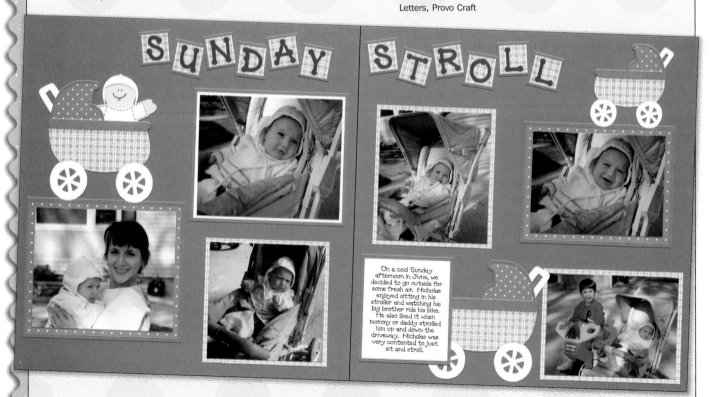

SUNDAY STROLL

On a cool Sunday
afternoon in June, we
decided to go outside for
some fresh air. Nicholas
enjoyed sitting in his
stroller and watching his
big brother ride his bike.
He also liked it when
mommy or daddy strolled
him up and down the
driveway. Nicholas was
very contented to just
sit and stroll.

Katie loved being a Big sister!
Rachael didn't mind the attention one bit...

"There Is Nothing Quite Like a Sister"

by Robin Johnson
Chandler, Arizona

SUPPLIES

Patterned paper: Mara-Mi;
Colors By Design (plaid)
Decorated die cuts: Cross My Heart
Page title: Bits & Pieces
Photo frame: Source unknown

There is nothing quite like a sister.

Sophia with great Grandpa Edwards
Easter Weekend 1998

"Tah Dah with Grandpa"

by Shauna Dunn
Springville, Utah

SUPPLIES

Patterned paper: The Paper Patch
Pen: Zig Clean Color, EK Success
Lettering template: Block, Pebble Tracers,
Pebbles in my Pocket

JOURNALING IDEA:

*Photograph your baby
interacting with special people
or items, such as playing
patty-cake with Mom or
cuddling with his or her
favorite toy or blanket.*

Sophia was pretty excited to be "standing!"
Great grandpa has done "tah-dahs" with three
generations of our family: grandma Sally, Mommy & now Sophia.

Paper edge: Corkscrew by Fiskars

"That's What Little Girlz Are Made Of"

by Heather Holdaway
Draper, Utah
SUPPLIES

Pens: Zig Writers, EK Success
Colored pencils: Prismacolor, Sanford
Patterned paper: Scrapable Scribbles (polka dot)
Girl: Heather adapted the idea from
a Scrapable Scribbles pattern.
Snail, rocks and grass: Heather's own designs

"Baby in the Cardboard Box"

by Brooke McLay
Colorado Springs, Colorado
SUPPLIES

Pens: Zig Writer and Zig Opaque Writer, EK Success
Colored pencils: Memory Pencils, EK Success

"Got Milk?"

by Pam Talluto
Rochester Hills, Michigan
SUPPLIES
Patterned paper: Provo Craft
Pen: Tombow
Computer font: Kidprint,
downloaded from
www.netpedia.com

Lettering template: Block,
Pebble Tracers,
Pebbles in my Pocket
Cow paper-piecing pattern:
Pam downloaded the pattern
from *www.gracefulbee.com*
on the Internet.
Milk bottle: Pam's own design

Paper edge: Corkscrew by Fiskars

"Parker in the Pumpkins"
by Jennifer Jensen
Hurricane, Utah
S U P P L I E S
Patterned paper: Over The Moon Press
(green plaid); Northern Spy (orange plaid)
Photo corners: D.O.T.S.
Pen: Zig Writer, EK Success
Scarecrow, pumpkins and fence:
Jennifer's own designs

"My Own Little Holly Hobbie"
by Pam Talluto
Rochester Hills, Michigan
S U P P L I E S
Patterned paper: Frances Meyer
Punches: Family Treasures
Pen: Tombow
Computer font: DJ Fancy, Fontastic!, D.J. Inkers
Lettering template: Block, Pebble Tracers,
Pebbles in my Pocket
Grass template: Pebble Tracers,
Pebbles in my Pocket

"Sometimes You Gotta Have a Nap"

by Vicki Garner
Windows of Time
Hooper, Utah

S U P P L I E S

Paper-piecing pattern: Baby Theme Pack,
Windows of Time
Computer font: Source unknown
Pen: Zig Writer, EK Success
Chalk: Craf-T Products

"How to Eat a Popsicle"

by Kim Heffington
Avondale, Arizona

S U P P L I E S

Patterned paper: Colors By Design
(blue); D.J. Inkers (orange)
Popsicle die cut: Ellison

Lettering idea: "Spiky Classic" from
The Art of Creative Lettering by
Creating Keepsakes Books
Colored pencils: Prismacolor, Sanford
Pen: Zig Writer, EK Success

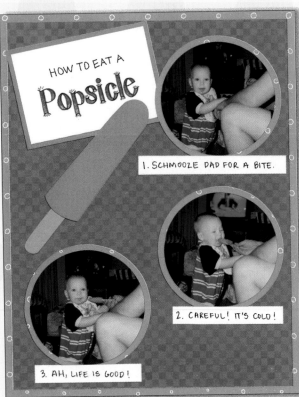

HOW TO EAT A
Popsicle

1. SCHMOOZE DAD FOR A BITE.

2. CAREFUL! IT'S COLD!

3. AH, LIFE IS GOOD!

"When I Grow Up"

by Kimberly Isaacson
Provo, Utah

S U P P L I E S

Patterned paper:
Keeping Memories Alive
Lettering template: Block, Pebble Tracers,
Pebbles in my Pocket
Post die cut: Pebbles in my Pocket
Paper doll: Kimberly's own design

Cowboy hat and boots template: Wild
West, Provo Craft
Corner star punch: Family Treasures
Hole punch: Family Treasures
Pen: Zig Millennium, EK Success
Colored pencils: Memory Pencils,
EK Success
Idea to note: Kimberly made the rope on
the hat by twisting a small strip of card-
stock every ¼ inch.

"Gone Fishin'"
by Marci Leishman
Draper, Utah
SUPPLIES
Scissors: Deckle edge, Family Treasures
Computer font: DJ Popsicle, Fontastic! 2, D.J. Inkers
Straw hat: Wang International
Clip art: Annette Ward, Provo Craft

Paper edge: Corkscrew by Fiskars

"Whirlwind"
by Alycia Alvarez
Altus, Oklahoma
SUPPLIES
Spiral punch: All Night Media
Pen: Zig Millennium, EK Success
Computer font: CK Anything Goes,
"The Best of Creative Lettering" CD Vol. 1, *Creating Keepsakes*

"Rachel Was Making a Big Splash"

by Jenny Jackson
Arlington, Virginia
SUPPLIES
Page title: Page Toppers, Cock-A-Doodle Design, Inc.
Scissors: Wavy Edge, Provo Craft
Pen: Scrapbook Writer, Close To My Heart

"Tyler '99"
by Nancy Church
Augusta, Georgia
SUPPLIES
Teardrop punch: Punchline, McGill
Lettering template: Block, Pebble Tracers,
Pebbles in my Pocket

"Beach Babies"
by Nancy Church
Augusta, Georgia
SUPPLIES
Patterned paper: Northern Spy
Hole punches: Punchline, McGill
Stickers: remember when . . ., Colorbök
Computer font: Scrap Kids, Lettering Delights,
Inspire Graphics
Lettering template: Puffy, Provo Craft

Paper edge: Corkscrew by Fiskars

Aunt Linda's corvette
Piedmont, CA.

Spring 1973

"Speed Racer"

by Emily Magleby
Springville, Utah

S U P P L I E S

Scissors: Deckle edge, Family Treasures
Punches: Family Treasures (large circle);
Marvy Uchida (small circle)
Doll die cut: Accu-Cut Systems
Pen: Micron Pigma, Sakura
Lettering template: Fat Lower, Frances Meyer
Car: Emily's own design

"Rainy Days"

by Kristina Nicolai-White
Two Peas in a Bucket
Middleton, Wisconsin

S U P P L I E S

Patterned paper: Frances Meyer
Die cuts: Stamping Station
(cloud); Accu-Cut Systems
(paper doll)

Punches: All Night Media (spiral
for hair); Family Treasures
(circle)
Pens: Zig Writer and Zig Opaque
Writer, EK Success
Alphabet letters: Kids,
Repositionable Sticky Die-Cut
Letters, Provo Craft
Wagon: Kristina's own design

rainy days
4.3.99
Arianna got a new wagon for Easter, from Grandma & Grandpa. we went to play with it the day before Easter - but it was all Rainy! Luckily, Arianna has a slicker - and she was able to go out-side!! she looks so cute in her slicker!!

Radio Flyer

Town & Country Wagon

Mommy pulls Arianna in her wagon for a walk.

Ari squeals "weeeee!"

Grandma shows Arianna the budding spring flowers.

On July 11, 1998, Sophiia "ran" (well, crawled) in her first race. Harmon's grocery store, Orem, Utah

Runners - Take Your Places!!

Sophia Isabella Dunn
9 months old.

"Speedy Sophia"

HUGGIES® Happy Baby Derby
21

® Registered trademark of Kimberly-Clark Corp.
Orem, UT ©1998, © 1998 WCC
©©-2014 Printed in U.S.A.

We almost didn't make it to the race. It was Daddy's birthday, and so we were having a fun morning at home, eating yummy birthday cheesecake for breakfast. We got to the store just in time to get Sophia into the last heat.

I love this picture of Sophia happy, yet highly determined outlook on life.

Sophia got a T-shirt & a bib from Huggies® We got a $25 gift certificate from Harmon's for participating. We bought children's books & tub toys.

START

On your marks, get set, CRAWL!
Sophia took off the starting line like a pro. Her "SideWinder" style allows her to move FAST! She was way out in front, and then realized "Hey! All these people are clapping and hollering for me!" She stopped and began waving and entertaining her enthusiastic audience.

And they're off...

Sophia didn't win the race, but if they would have had a category for "Most original style" our Fia would have been the hands-down champion!

Sophia crawls with her left hand and leg (what I call her "left-foot First" speed). Sometimes she drags her left foot left pretty tast. She has bent up her center her left leg callus on.

"Our Little Champion"

Racing to the Finish Line.

FINISH

We took these pictures after the actual race. Sophia certainly played to the camera. She whizzed to the Finish line. Maybe we will do this again and practice beforehand... Sophia definitely has what it takes! What a champ.

Let's do that again! It was FUN!

"Start ... Finish"
by Shauna Dunn
Springville, Utah
SUPPLIES
Pen: Zig Writer, EK Success
"Start" and "finish": From the baby derby
Other: Shauna included portions of the contest waiver and announcement on the layout.

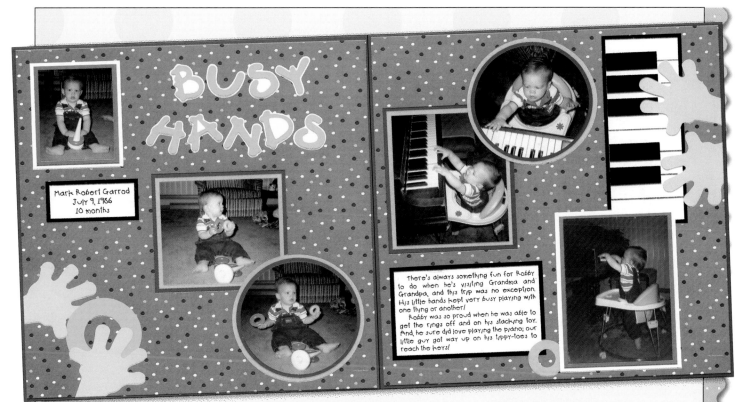

"Busy Hands"
by Sally Garrod
East Lansing, Michigan
SUPPLIES

Patterned paper: The Paper Patch
Circle punches: Family Treasures
Lettering template (scanned and enlarged):
Kids, Provo Craft
Computer font: DJ Crayon, Fontastic!,
D.J. Inkers
Hands template: "Baby, Baby," Provo Craft
Piano and toy rings: Sally's own designs
Other: Sally used shiny paper to make
the piano look more realistic.

"Silly Boy"
by Kim Heffington
Puzzle Mates
Brea, California
SUPPLIES

Patterned paper: Paper Adventures
Lettering idea: "Stitches" from
The Art of Creative Lettering by
Creating Keepsakes Books
Puzzle template: Oval, Puzzle Mates
Colored pencils: Prismacolor, Sanford
Pen: Zig Writer, EK Success

"It Don't Mean a Thing if It Ain't Got That Swing"

by Heidi Allen
Everett, Washington

SUPPLIES

Letter stickers: K & Company
Pens: Zig Writer and Zig Millennium,
EK Success; Crystal Point, Marvy Uchida
Colored pencils: Prismacolor, Sanford
Lettering template (chain on swing):
Ol' Calhoon, D.O.T.S.
Templates: Picket, D.J. Inkers (flowers); School,
Pebble Tracers, Pebbles in my Pocket (grass, leaves)

"You Can Learn a Lot of Things from the Flowers

by Keisha Reshay Lowe
Macon, Georgia

SUPPLIES

Patterned paper: Frances Meyer (flowers);
Paperbilities, MPR (doll dress)
Sun: Little Bits, The Gick Co.
Paper doll: Stick People, Stamping Station
Stickers: Frances Meyer (flowers and butterflies);
Stickopotamus (flowers on doll dress)
Pen: Zig Millennium, EK Success

A baby girl's world is
soft with lullabies,
sweet with hugs,
bright with wonder,
warm with love.

"May '99"

by Keisha Reshay Lowe
Macon, Georgia
SUPPLIES
Patterned paper: The Paper Patch
Pre-pasted flower die cut: Wallies

Alphabet letters: Fat Dot,
Repositionable Sticky Die-Cut
Letters, Provo Craft
Idea to note: Keisha used a
poem from a Hallmark greeting
card on the layout.

"Growing by Leaps and Bounds"

by Desirée Tanner
Provo Craft
Provo, Utah
SUPPLIES
Patterned paper: The Paper Patch
Lettering template: Rounded Serif,
Pebble Tracers, Pebbles in my Pocket
Stickers: Provo Craft
Scissors: Ripple edge, Fiskars
Pen: Zig Millennium, EK Success

Adrien
and the
Purple Crayon

16 months
old

Adrien found a
purple crayon and
like Harold he began
to draw on everything
in sight. He even made
the letter A!

"Adrien and the Purple Crayon"

Kimberly Smith
Reddick, Florida
SUPPLIES
Patterned paper: The Paper Patch
Scissors: Deckle edge, Fiskars
Pens: Zig Millennium, EK Success;
Hybrid Gel Roller, Marvy Uchida

Die cuts: Ellison
Idea to note: Kimberly color-
copied the "Harold and the
Purple Crayon" image from a
children's book.

Paper edge: Corkscrew by Fiskars

One of McKenna's favorite things at Grandma & Grandpa Mitchell's is the swing! She always squeals with delight as she swings higher and higher! For a while, she would only let Uncle T.J. push her in the swing... boy, did he love that! McKenna is getting so big! She's already 19 months old!

CLINTON, UTAH

September 1999

"Swingin'"

by Brenda Bennett
Morenci, Arizona
SUPPLIES
Patterned paper (grass): Paper Pizazz, Hot Off The Press
Lettering template: Kids, Provo Craft
Computer font: DJ Crayon, Fontastic!, D.J. Inkers
Grass die cut: Brenda's own design
Other: Brenda tore the paper to make the tree, leaves, clouds and rope.

"McAllister Park"

by Erin Terrell
San Antonio, Texas
SUPPLIES
Lettering template: Block Serif, Pebble Tracers, Pebbles in my Pocket
Paper-piecing pattern (modified): Amusement Park, Scrapable Scribbles
Computer font: DJ FiddleSticks, FiddleSticks, D.J. Inkers
Hole punch: Punchline, McGill
Pens: Zig Writers, EK Success
Slide, sandbox, bucket, ball and clothes: Erin's own designs
Idea to note: Erin used sandpaper for the sand in the sandbox.

We took Daisy to the park one Sunday because she wasn't feeling too well. We needed a good distraction! She ended up having a great time playing on the slide with her daddy and getting dirty in the sand! Mission Accomplished!

"Makin' Wishes"

by Kerri Bradford
Orem, Utah
SUPPLIES
Patterned paper: Colors By Design (green scribble, blue checked); Robin's Nest (yellow circle); Paperbilities, MPR (pink plaid)
Alphabet letters: Kids, Repositionable Sticky Die-Cut Letters, Provo Craft
Stickers: Suzy's Zoo
Pens: Zig Writers, EK Success

Brevin spends a beautiful summer day outside with mom, just hangin' out and eating an occasional flower or two!
11 months old

she luvs me...

she luvs me not...

Hmmm...this looks rather interesting. I'd better take a closer look. I kinda like how it looks and feels...

It's really quite pretty & smells good too.

Here Mom, I think that this is something you might like.

Isaac, July '96

"She Luvs Me ... She Luvs Me Not"

by Kristy Banks
Highland, Utah
SUPPLIES
Daisy die cuts:
Pebbles in my Pocket
Computer fonts: CK Anything Goes, "The Best of Creative Lettering" CD Vol. 1, *Creating Keepsakes*; Scrap Swirl, Lettering Delights, Inspire Graphics

Leaf and circle punches:
Family Treasures
Hole punch: Punchline, McGill
Colored pencils: Memory Pencils, EK Success
Ladybugs: Kristy's own designs
Idea to note: Kristy used the Kodak Picture Maker to enlarge her photos.

"Here, Mom"

by Jodi Olson
Redmond, Washington
SUPPLIES
Patterned paper: GeoPapers
Punches: Marvy Uchida (small daisy); Family Treasures (large daisy); McGill (bow border)
Pen: Micron Pigma, Sakura
Specialty paper: Paper Cuts (vellum paper)
Idea to note: Jodi layered a vellum daisy over a white cardstock daisy to add dimension.

"Adrienne Loves Her Dolly"

by Sally Garrod
East Lansing, Michigan
SUPPLIES
Patterned paper: Frances Meyer
Scissors: Deckle, Mini-Scallop
and Scallop edges, Fiskars
Punches: Family Treasures
(circle); All Night Media (spiral)

Hole punch: Punchline, McGill
Doll die cut: Accu-Cut Systems
Computer font: DJ Fancy,
Fontastic!, D.J. Inkers
Idea to note: Sally dressed the
doll die cut to look like her
daughter's doll.

"Fuzzy Friends"

by Karen Towery
Dallas, Georgia
SUPPLIES
Computer font: DJ HomeMade, Fontastic!, D.J. Inkers
Stickers: Sandylion (small animals); Frances Meyer (pawprints)
Scissors: Deckle edge, Fiskars
Pen: Zig Writer, EK Success

Arianna just adores her Noopy. She demands that he sleep next to her everynight! She refuses to get out of bed in the morning until he is firmly tucked beneath her arm! He is definitely a favorite lovey!

Her "B"s are also favorite loveys! She has 4. 2 white & 2 green. They are a must have - no matter where we go. (1-10-99) (2-11-99)

"Noopy, B & Me"

by Kristina Nicolai-White
Two Peas in a Bucket
Middleton, Wisconsin
SUPPLIES
Patterned paper: Northern Spy (plaid); Keeping Memories Alive (speckled)
Specialty papers: Wintech (Vivelle plush paper); Paper Adventures (velveteen paper)
Pen: Zig Millennium, EK Success
Lettering template: Rounded Serif, Pebble Tracers, Pebbles in my Pocket

"Binky Boy"

by Kim Heffington
Avondale, Arizona
SUPPLIES
Patterned paper: Provo Craft
Specialty paper: Paper Cuts (vellum paper)
Punches: McGill (jumbo circle); Acco (circle); All Night Media (mini-spiral)
Hole punch: Punchline, McGill
Pens: Micron Pigma, Sakura; Zig Writers, EK Success
Lettering idea: "Choppy Block" from *The Art of Creative Lettering* by Creating Keepsakes Books

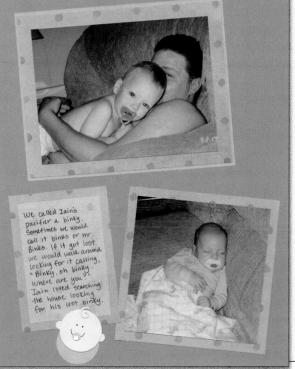

We called Iain's pacifier a binky. Sometimes we would call it binks or mr. Binks. If it got lost we would walk around looking for it calling "Binky, oh binky, where are you?" Iain loved searching the house looking for his lost binky.

"Two Little Monkeys"

by Desirée Tanner
Provo Craft
Provo, Utah

S U P P L I E S

Patterned paper: The Paper Patch
Monkey sticker: Provo Craft
Bananas: Desirée's own designs

"Yep, I'm 100% Pure Girl ..."

by Erin Terrell
San Antonio, Texas

S U P P L I E S

Patterned paper:
Keeping Memories Alive
Watermelon die cuts: Cindy
Lettering template:
Block Serif, Pebble Tracers,
Pebbles in my Pocket

Computer font: CK Script,
"The Best of Creative
Lettering" CD Vol. 1,
Creating Keepsakes
Pens: Zig Writers,
EK Success
Girl: Erin's own design
Other: Erin included
"googly" eyes and ribbon
on the layout.

I don't move my arms when I walk or run so I look like a little gorilla. I am gentle and loving. I love cheese puffs. My very favorite foods are apricots and plums. I weigh 28 lbs. I am 11 months old.

Daisy's latest creation:

Mix:
• 1 part sweat
• 1 part dirt (and don't be stingy with it!) and
• the juice from one watermelon

What do you get? One REALLY yucky little girl!!

I took these pictures one really hot day in August. Daisy was covered in dirt and sweat. I figured – why not add to it and give her a watermelon? Afterwards – she went straight to the tub!

Yep
I'm 100% pure
girl...
just don't expect me
to always LOOK
the part!!

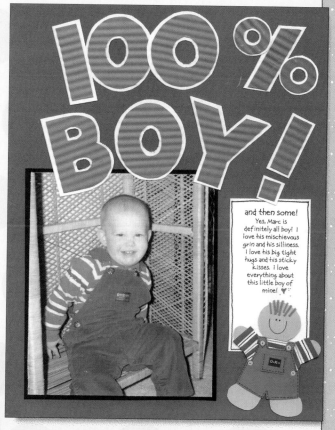

"Hello"
by Kim Heffington
Avondale, Arizona
SUPPLIES
Patterned paper: Colors By Design
Lettering template: Ol' Calhoon, D.O.T.S.
Pen: Micron Pigma, Sakura

BAGEL GOT A NEW BONE FOR CHRISTMAS & IAIN THOUGHT IT LOOKED JUST LIKE A TELEPHONE. HE HELD IT UP TO HIS EAR & WALKED AROUND SAYING, "HELLO...".
DECEMBER 1995

and then some!
Yes, Marc is definitely all boy! I love his mischievous grin and his silliness. I love his big tight hugs and his sticky kisses. I love everything about this little boy of mine! ♥

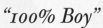

January 1999

Paper edge: Corkscrew by Fiskars

"100% Boy"
by Pam Talluto
Rochester Hills, Michigan
SUPPLIES
Lettering template: Block, Pebble Tracers, Pebbles in my Pocket
Computer font: Kidprint, downloaded from www.netpedia.com
Crimper: Fiskars
Gingerbread-boy template: Christmas, Pebble Tracers, Pebbles in my Pocket
Hole punch: Punchline, McGill
Pen: Tombow
Doll clothes: Pam's own designs

"Skating with Sophia"
by Shauna Dunn
Springville, Utah
SUPPLIES
Punches: Family Treasures (large flower); McGill (medium-flower corner punch)
Doll die cut: Accu-Cut Systems
Pen: Milky Gel Roller, Pentel
Doll clothes: Shauna's own designs

"Sweetest Heart"

by Shauna Dunn
Springville, Utah
SUPPLIES
Patterned paper: The Paper Patch
Page title: Page Toppers, Cock-A-Doodle Design, Inc.
Pen: Milky Gel Roller, Pentel

"Craig the Conqueror"

by Rebecca Jahnke
Lancaster, Pennsylvania
SUPPLIES

Computer font (title): Sherwood Regular, Print Artist

Helmet: Print Artist

Specialty paper: Personal Stamp Exchange (mulberry paper)

Pens: Zig Writers, EK Success; Writing and Drawing Pen, Fiskars

Boat: Rebecca's own design

How we love our sweet Fia
July 1999

"Flower Girl"
by Erin Terrell
San Antonio, Texas
SUPPLIES
Patterned paper: The Paper Patch
Daisy punch: Family Treasures
Flower template: Provo Craft
Computer fonts: CK Script and CK Anything Goes,
"The Best of Creative Lettering" CD Vol. 1,
Creating Keepsakes
Pen: Zig Writer, EK Success
Colored pencils: Prismacolor, Sanford

"You Quack Me Up"
by Pam Talluto
Rochester Hills, Michigan
SUPPLIES
Patterned paper: Pixie Press
Lettering template: Block, Pebble Tracers,
Pebbles in my Pocket
Scissors: Scallop edge, Fiskars
Punches: Family Treasures
Pen: Zig Writer, EK Success
Other: Pam got the idea for the ducks
from *Punchin'* by Design Originals.

Paper edge: Corkscrew by Fiskars

"Just the Girls"
by Cheryl Souter
Scrapbooker's Paradise
Calgary, Alberta, Canada
SUPPLIES
Patterned paper: NRN Designs
Specialty paper: Craf-T Pedlar (handmade paper)
Hole punches: Punchline, McGill
Punches: Family Treasures (large daisy);
Marvy Uchida (small daisy)
Lettering template: Classic Caps,
Frances Meyer

"Our Little Rosebud"
by Lori Bergmann
Turlock, California
SUPPLIES
Patterned paper: Over The Moon Press
Die cuts: Over The Moon Press
Pen: Zig Opaque Writer, EK Success

"Baby, Oh Baby"
by Marcia Cornell
My Mind's Eye
Bountiful, Utah
SUPPLIES
Patterned paper: NRN Designs
Decorated die cuts: My Mind's Eye
Decorated frame: Frame-Ups, My Mind's Eye
Page title: My Mind's Eye
Pen: Zig Writer, EK Success

"Mommy's Little Angel"

by Shauna Devereux
Athens, Georgia

S U P P L I E S

Patterned paper: Provo Craft

Paper-piecing pattern: Shauna got the idea from a Windows of Time pattern.

Cloud embossing template: Wacky shapes, Frances Meyer

Doll die cut: Stamping Station

Specialty paper: The Paper Company (vellum paper)

Watercolor pencils: Derwent

Computer font: CK Script, "The Best of Creative Lettering" CD Vol. 1, Creating Keepsakes

Pen: Zig Millennium, EK Success

Hole punch: Punchline, McGill

"I'm Growing Up!"

by Marcia Cornell
My Mind's Eye
Bountiful, Utah

S U P P L I E S

Patterned paper: The Paper Patch

Decorated die cuts: My Mind's Eye

Page title: My Mind's Eye

Decorated frame: Frame-Ups, My Mind's Eye

Specialty paper: Paper Cuts (vellum paper)

Pen: Zig Writer, EK Success

Idea to note: Marcia used vellum to make a pocket page, which holds notes from her baby's visits to the doctor.

Paper edge: Corkscrew by Fiskars

It's official! James Glenn Snyder weighs in at 18 lbs. 6 oz. according to postal employee and Grandfather Glenn Dale Mumford.

Mom, Nichole and James visiting Grandpa at work.

Central Point, Oregon
June, 1988

U.S. MALE

"U.S. Male"
by Michelle Snyder
Nampa, Idaho
SUPPLIES

Lettering template: Dream Talk, D.O.T.S.
Pen: Legacy Writer, D.O.T.S.
Idea to note: Michelle made a color copy
of the badge from the U.S. Post Office and
included it on her layout.

"Wheel of Fortune"
by Pam Talluto
Rochester Hills, Michigan
SUPPLIES

Lettering template: Block, Pebble Tracers,
Pebbles in my Pocket
Computer font: Arial, Microsoft Word
Pen: Milky Gel Roller, Pentel
"Wheel of Fortune": Pam's own design

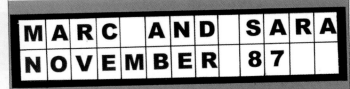

MARC AND SARA
NOVEMBER 87

"Zach in a Box"

by Jenny Jackson
Arlington, Virginia
S U P P L I E S

Patterned paper: Frances Meyer
Computer font: Beesknees ITC and
Times New Roman, Microsoft Word
Jack-in-the-box: Jenny's own design

When we lived in El Paso, TX in our little apartment, Zach would spend hours at a time emptying & filling his toy basket. He thought it was so funny to climb inside with the toys! Zach is a happy baby!!

"Too Dog-Gone Cute"

by Vicki Garner
Windows of Time
Hooper, Utah
S U P P L I E S

Paper-piecing pattern: Hot Digity Dog, Windows of Time
Patterned paper: The Paper Patch
Computer font: Comic Sans MS, Print Artist

TOO "DOG GONE" CUTE

Oh Boy! I love hats. Playing with Aunt Desiree's hat was a blast.

"First Kisses"

by Cheryl Souter
Scrapbooker's Paradise
Calgary, Alberta, Canada
S U P P L I E S

Patterned paper: Provo Craft
Specialty paper: Wintech (Vivelle plush paper)
Lettering template: Fat Caps, Frances Meyer
Pen: Zig Writer, EK Success

Braydon and Savanna, the little girl I babysat, having lunch. She was a very lovey baby, with lots of hugs and kisses for everyone. ~ June '98

Paper edge: Corkscrew by Fiskars

"Austin's Favorite Foods"
by Marilyn Healey
West Jordan, Utah
SUPPLIES
Stationery: MM's Design
Pens: Micron Pigma, Sakura; Zig Writer, EK Success

Austin at 18 months

He likes cheese, yogurt, grapes, pizza, bananas, apples, spaghetti, black beans, tomatoes, french fries, peanutbutter sandwiches, and drinking from a cup.

Austin doesn't like peaches, strawberries and baloney sandwiches.

"Sophia Is a Cookie Monster"
by Shauna Dunn
Springville, Utah
SUPPLIES
Puzzle template: Puzzle Mates
Sticker: Source unknown
Cookie monster: Shauna's own design

September 1998   Eleven Months Old

~Cookie Monster~

Cookie Monster

Sophia's First Oreo Cookie was a huge hit!

Sophia is a Cookie Monster.

September 1998 ... Eleven Months Old

"Queen of Cooking (and Tasting)"

by Heather Holdaway Thatcher
Draper, Utah

S U P P L I E S

Patterned paper: Close To My Heart/D.O.T.S. (pink and blue polka dot, pink gingham); Frances Meyer (plaid); Northern Spy (blue and pink plaid); The Paper Patch (periwinkle polka dot)

Chalk: Craf-T Products

Colored pencils: Prismacolor, Sanford

Pens: Zig Writers, EK Success

Lettering, dough, rolling pins and babies: Heather's own designs

"A Kid Who Doesn't Like Ice Cream?"

by Jodi Olson
Redmond, Washington

S U P P L I E S

Alphabet letters: Alphabitties, Repositionable Sticky Die-Cut Letters, Provo Craft

Pen: Zig Writer, EK Success

Ice cream cones: Jodi's own designs

"Skyler Loves Ice Cream"

by Shannon Lowe
Salt Lake City, Utah

S U P P L I E S

Patterned paper: The Paper Patch

Computer font: DJ Crayon, Fontastic!, D.J. Inkers

Sticker: Mrs. Grossman's

Other: Shannon tore paper to make the picture frames and ice cream cone.

Paper edge: Corkscrew by Fiskars

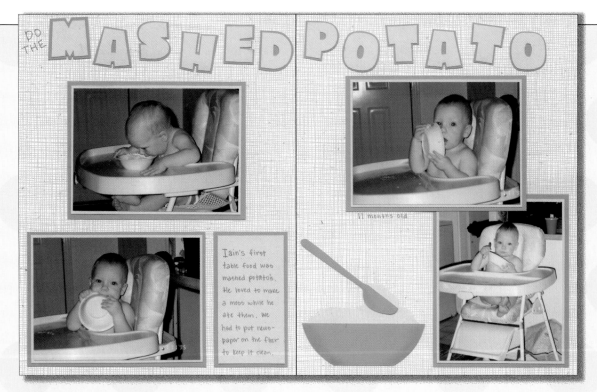

Iain's first table food was mashed potato's. He loved to make a mess while he ate them. We had to put newspaper on the floor to keep it clean.

11 months old

"Do the Mashed Potato"
by Kim Heffington
Avondale, Arizona
SUPPLIES
Patterned paper: Northern Spy
Spoon template: Pebble Tracers, Pebbles in my Pocket
Pen: Zig Writer, EK Success
Lettering template: Fat Caps, Frances Meyer
Chalk (on bowl and potatoes): Craf-T Products

"Yummy Pasta"
by Diane Garding
North Bend, Washington
SUPPLIES
Heart punch: Family Treasures
Pen: Zig Writer, EK Success
Lettering template: Wacky, Frances Meyer

Pasta paper: Diane made her own pasta patterned paper by scanning pasta using her computer and printing it out.

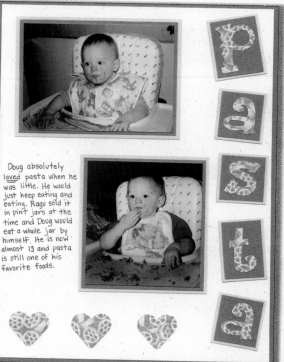

Doug absolutely loved pasta when he was little. He would just keep eating and eating. Ragu sold it in pint jars at the time and Doug would eat a whole jar by himself. He is now almost 13 and pasta is still one of his favorite foods.

It's hard to be

N E A T ...

When you're learning to

E A T !

Hannah
Summer '97

"It's Hard to Be Neat ..."
by Pam Talluto
Rochester Hills, Michigan
SUPPLIES
Patterned paper: The Paper Patch
Spiral punch: All Night Media
Computer fonts: CK Toggle and CK Boxes,
"The Best of Creative Lettering" CD Vol. 2,
Creating Keepsakes

"Me Want Cookies"
by Kim Heffington
Avondale, Arizona
SUPPLIES
Patterned paper: Keeping Memories Alive
Circle punch: McGill
Hole punch: Punchline, McGill
Pen: Micron Pigma, Sakura
Lettering template: Fat Caps, Frances Meyer

ME WANT

C KIES

On may 18, 1995 we
discovered that Iain
loves cookies. He had
so much fun making

Such a big mess.
When the cookie was
finally gone - out came
the washcloth to

Clean up the mess.
As you can see,
Iain tried to eat
the washcloth too!

Paper edge: Corkscrew by Fiskars

"My Crib"

by Alycia Alvarez
Altus, Oklahoma

SUPPLIES

Crib die cut: Pebbles in my Pocket
Baby and blanket: Alycia's own designs
Corner lace punch: Tear Drop, Family Treasures
Letter stickers: Frances Meyer
Punches: Marvy Uchida (heart);
All Night Media (spiral); McGill (circle)
Hole punches: Punchline, McGill
Pens: Milky Gel Roller, Pentel;
Zig Writer, EK Success

"Two Darned Cute"

by Brooke McLay
Colorado Springs, Colorado

SUPPLIES

Patterned paper: Action Papers
Animal template: Perfect Pets,
Provo Craft

Scissors: Wave edge, Provo Craft
Pen: Zig Writer, EK Success
Colored pencils: Memory Pencils,
EK Success
Ark and title: Brooke's own designs

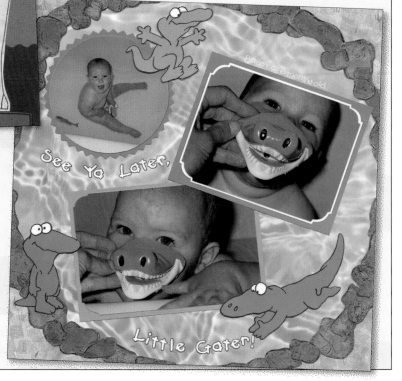

"See Ya Later, Little Gater!"

by Desirée Tanner
Provo Craft
Provo, Utah

SUPPLIES

Patterned paper: Provo Craft
Alphabet letters: Alphabitties, Repositionable
Sticky Die-Cut Letters, Provo Craft
Corner punch: Southwest, McGill
Scissors: Pinking edge, Fiskars
Alligator die cuts: Desirée's own designs
Pens: Zig Writer, EK Success;
Milky Gel Roller, Pentel

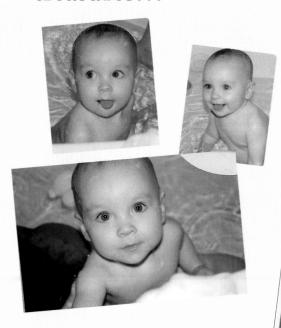

from shoeboxes *to* family treasures...

We'll show you how!

Discover the pleasure of creating a family treasure!

Whether you're a beginning scrapbooker or a seasoned pro, *Creating Keepsakes* scrapbook magazine has everything you need to organize and creatively present your treasured memories. You don't need a lot of time, talent or money to get started! It's fun using archival papers and today's new specialized scrapbooking products. Enjoy the new product reviews and experiment with

techniques from the experts. You'll love our Creative Lettering column with easy-to-follow instructions. Plus, each issue is jam packed with oodles of fantastic scrapbook page examples. Start organizing and preserving your family's memories to last through the generations with a little help from the recognized scrapbooking authority— *Creating Keepsakes* scrapbook magazine!

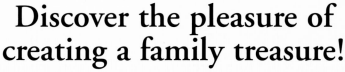

Send for Your FREE Issue Today!
Don't let your precious memories fade away.

CREATING
Keepsakes
SCRAPBOOK MAGAZINE

The Scrapbooking Authority!

B00AA-5

"ZZZ"

by Erin Terrell
San Antonio, Texas
SUPPLIES
Patterned paper: Keeping Memories Alive
(speckled); Lasting Impressions (checked,
polka dot)
Arrow template: Funky, Provo Craft
Computer font: CK Script,
"The Best of Creative Lettering" CD Vol. 1,

Creating Keepsakes
Pens: Zig Writer, EK Success;
Milky Gel Roller, Pentel
Colored pencils: Prismacolor, Sanford
Hole punch: Punchline, McGill
Baby face: Erin's own design
Other: Erin made her own background
paper on the title by dotting the paper
with a pen.

"A Pot Full of Fun"

by Sally Garrod
East Lansing, Michigan
SUPPLIES
Patterned paper: The Paper Patch
Punches: Family Treasures
Hole punch: Punchline, McGill
Die cuts: Accu-Cut Systems
Stickers: PrintWorks (white lines);
Mrs. Grossman's (bear)

Colored pencils: Prismacolor,
Sanford
Computer font: DJ Squared,
Fantastic!, D.J. Inkers
Pots: Sally's own designs
Other: Sally scanned and
enlarged her photos.
Idea to note: Sally used shiny
paper to make the pots look
more realistic.

"Cute Things"
by Jennifer McLaughlin
Back Door Friends—The Scrapbooking
Company
Whittier, California
SUPPLIES
Patterned paper: Frances Meyer (hearts);
Jenny Faw Designs (flowers)
Computer font: CK Toggle,
"The Best of Creative Lettering" CD Vol. 2,
Creating Keepsakes
Pen: Zig Writer, EK Success
Colored pencils: Prismacolor, Sanford

"I Love Books"
by Karen Towery
Dallas, Georgia
SUPPLIES
Patterned paper: Sonburn
Letter die cuts: Dayco
Rotary trimmer: Deckle edge, Fiskars
Star corner punch: Family Treasures
Computer font: CK Print, "The Best of Creative
Lettering" CD Vol. 1, *Creating Keepsakes*

Jack likes to pick out books and bring them to Mommy or Daddy to read. He says "okay!" and climbs up into our lap. He likes to point out the sun, moon, stars, cows, bunnies and puppies. He always laughs at Mommy's dramatic reading and Daddy's silly sound effects. Pictured on these pages are many of Jack's favorites.

Paper edge: Corkscrew by Fiskars

"Uh, Oh"
by Jana Francis
Provo, Utah
SUPPLIES
Patterned paper: Close To My Heart/D.O.T.S.
Pen: Zig Writer, EK Success
Toilet and letters: Jana's own designs

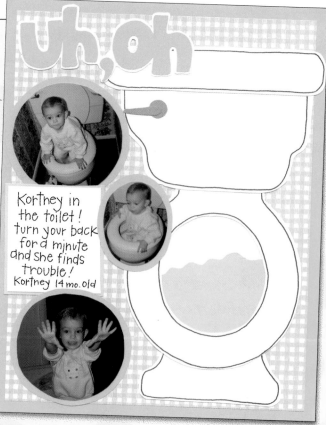

Kortney in the toilet! turn your back for a minute and she finds trouble!
Kortney 14 mo. old

September 1991

I came downstairs this day to find my little lovin' playing gleefully in a huge pile of toilet paper! She thought she was so clever! It was a very cheap toy at 25 cents per roll!

"Potty Paper"
by Lynnette Carruthers
Belvidere, Illinois
SUPPLIES
Patterned paper: The Paper Patch
Scissors: Pinking edge, Fiskars
Pen: Gelly Roll, Sakura
Chalk: Craf-T Products
Colored pencils: Prismacolor, Sanford
Toilet paper roll and flower paper:
Lynnette's own designs

"Peek-a-Boo"
by Sharon Lewis
Memory Lane
Mesa, Arizona
SUPPLIES
Patterned paper: The Paper Patch
Specialty paper: Penny Black (vellum paper)
Punches: Family Treasures
Pens: Micron Pigma, Sakura
Colored pencils: Memory Pencils, EK Success
Lettering idea: "Happy Kids" from
The Art of Creative Lettering by
Creating Keepsakes Books
Other: Sharon used raffia on her layout.

My most favorite game!

Juliette ~ Spring 1995

Trey Briggs Sept. '98 - Feb. '99

Suits me

we love to give you a bath.. and then dress you in one of your cute outfits. when your brothers get involved... it's a photo shoot for sure.

just fine.

my snow suit.

my swimming suit.

given to you by melissa burbank

my birthday suit.

handsewn by Tenrie Clancy

my bear suit.

mom cant decide... are you cuter with.. or - without clothes?

my santa suit.

my clown suit.

"Suits Me Just Fine"
by Stacy Julian
Lewiston, Idaho
SUPPLIES

Lettering template: Block, Pebble Tracers, Pebbles in my Pocket
Chalk: Craf-T Products
Stickers: Bryce & Madeline, remember when . . ., Colorbök
Pen: Gelly Roll, Sakura

"Playtime with Daddy and Sarah"
by Sally Garrod
East Lansing, Michigan
SUPPLIES

Patterned paper: Memory Press
Daisy and leaf punches: Family Treasures
Teardrop and hole punches: Punchline, McGill
Heart die cuts: Creative Memories
Computer font: Scrap Marker, Lettering Delights, Inspire Graphics
Food and petal templates: Pebble Tracers, Pebbles in my Pocket

PLAYTIME WITH DADDY and SARAH

Daddy and Sarah had a happy time together playing the "Hat Game." Daddy would put his baseball cap on Sarah and she would laugh & giggle and pull it off and hand it back to him . . . again and again!

That orange mark on Sarah's cheek is leftover peaches just NHO cleaned her up after dinner anyway ???

Sarah Grace
7 months
March 22, 1998

Paper edge: Corkscrew by Fiskars

"Everywhere in Only Just My Underwear!"

by Jana Francis
Provo, Utah
SUPPLIES
Patterned paper: Close To My Heart/D.O.T.S.
Pen: Zig Fine & Chisel, EK Success
Underwear: Jana's own designs

"Beach Bum"

by Emily Magleby
Springville, Utah
SUPPLIES
Patterned paper: The Paper Patch (plaid);
Provo Craft (sand)
Pen: Micron Pigma, Sakura
Lettering template: Block, Pebble Tracers,
Pebbles in my Pocket
Umbrella: Emily's own design

"Piggy Tails"

by Jana Francis
Provo, Utah
SUPPLIES
Patterned paper: The Paper Patch
Pen: Zig Fine & Chisel, EK Success
Hair: Jana's own design

"Who Needs Toys When You Have a Sister?"

by Denise Stott
Mom and Me Scrapbooking
Salt Lake City, Utah
SUPPLIES
Scissors: Scallop edge, Fiskars
Punches: Family Treasures (car, scallop, teddy
bear, rabbit, tea pot, cup); McGill (bow, circles);
McGill (teardrop, hole, flower, oval, star, circle,
square); Marvy Uchida (sun, tulip); Rubber
Stampede (Mickey Mouse)
Die cuts: Ellison (bucket); Accu-Cut Systems
(paper doll)
Pen: Gelly Roll, Sakura
Computer font: Scrap Marker, Lettering
Delights, Inspire Graphics
Xylophone, stick horse and boat: Denise's
own designs

"Color Me Happy"

by Heidi Allen
Everett, Washington
SUPPLIES
Pens: Zig Writer and Zig Scroll & Brush,
EK Success; Crystal Point, Marvy Uchida
Lettering template: Fat Caps,
Frances Meyer
Template: Border Buddy #3, EK Success

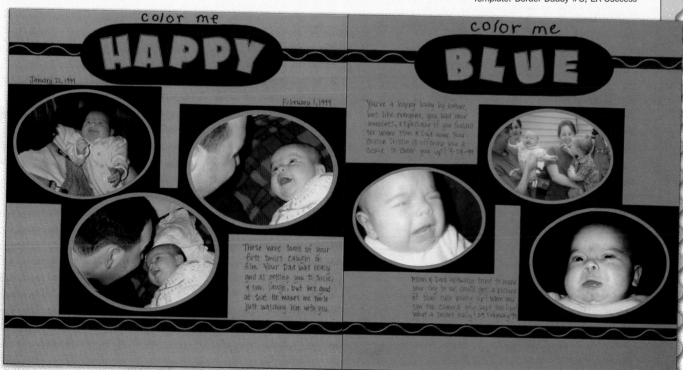

Paper edge: Corkscrew by Fiskars

My mommy likes Anne Gedde's photographs
Of babies and my Grandma likes snowmen – the perfect combination?
Anne Gedde's snowman pattern and Grandma's sewing machine.
Voila! Our family Christmas card
Featuring
Mister Nigel – Snowman Extraordinaire!

Mister Nigel,
Grandma's Favorite
Snowman!

Come, catch some falling snowflakes
Beside a country lane
Where we can make a snowman
with derby hat and cane...
from Simple Things by Amy Kartman

Snowmen Melt Your Heart

Nigel's 2nd Christmas, 1998

"Snowmen Melt Your Heart"

by Judi Lindgren
Between the Pages
Northbrook, Illinois

SUPPLIES

Patterned paper: Keeping Memories Alive

Punches: McGill

Computer font: Source unknown

Suns and borders: Judi's own designs

"Baby-Face Charly"

by Lori Allred
Your Country Peddler
Layton, Utah

SUPPLIES

Page title: Page Toppers,
Cock-A-Doodle Design, Inc.

Scissors: Pinking edge, Fiskars

Chalk: Craf-T Products

Stickers: Provo Craft

Pen: Zig Writer, EK Success

Baby and lettering: Lori's own designs

baby face

Charly

From Oo's to Ahh's,
Charly has always loved
posing for the camera! She
is only 9 months.

NOV. 1998

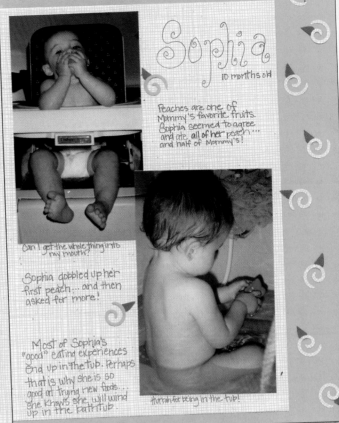

Peachy

Keen

Sophia
10 months old

Peaches are one of
Mommy's favorite fruits.
Sophia seemed to agree
and ate all of her peach ...
and half of Mommy's!

Can I get the whole thing into
my mouth?

Sophia gobbled up her
first peach ... and then
asked for more!

Most of Sophia's
"good" eating experiences
end up in the tub. Perhaps
that is why she is so
good at trying new foods ...
she knows she will wind
up in the bathtub.

Hurrah for being in the tub!

Sophia August 1998

"Peachy Keen"
by **Shauna Dunn**
Springville, Utah
S U P P L I E S
Patterned paper: Northern Spy
Lettering template: Block Serif,
Pebble Tracers, Pebbles in my Pocket
Punches: Family Treasures

The End

of Daisy's 1st Year

"The End"
by **Erin Terrell**
San Antonio, Texas
S U P P L I E S
Patterned paper: The Paper Patch
Daisy punch: Family Treasures
Hole punch: Punchline, McGill
Letter stickers: Frances Meyer
Lettering template: Block Serif, Pebble Tracers,
Pebbles in my Pocket
Pen: Zig Writer, EK Success

Paper edge: Corkscrew by Fiskars

by Heather Thatcher

Try Our Sweet Dreams Alphabet

Rock your little one to sleep with this cuddly alphabet

AFTER HAVING A BABY, YOUR RESTFUL nights usually turn into restless ones! While you're up at night, give our Sweet Dreams Alphabet a try (Figure 1). It's sure to give your baby photos the soft and dreamy touch they deserve. Read on to learn how to get the same fun look yourself.

CREATING THE SWEET DREAMS ALPHABET

To create the Sweet Dreams Alphabet, follow four quick steps:

❶ Using a pencil, write the word or phrase. Be sure to leave a little space between your letters. *Note:* I've found that this alphabet works best with capital letters, which tend to be more readable (Figure 2).

❷ Still using a pencil, outline each letter with bumps or "cloud-shaped" designs. You can add variety to your title by varying the puffy curves of the "clouds" on each letter—try short or long curves, or a combination of both. You might also want to vary the widths of the letters to add dimension to your lettering. Next, if your title calls for it, add stars and half-moons to your letters.

❸ Once you've written the word the way you like it, outline the stars, moons and let-

Figure 1. The Sweet Dreams Alphabet is a wonderful way to herald your newest addition. *Page by Heather Holdaway Thatcher.* **Supplies** *Patterned paper:* PrintWorks (striped); Wübie Prints (clouds); Source unknown (stars); *Vellum:* Sonburn; *Pen:* Zig Writer, EK Success; *Colored pencils:* Prismacolor, Sanford. *Idea to note:* Heather used yellow cardstock to "stitch" around some of the photo mats.

Step by Step

❶ Write your word in pencil.

❷ Still using pencil, enhance the letter by adding puffy curves. Add half-moons and stars to your design if desired.

❸ Outline the letter and enhancements with a pen.

❹ Color in the design to coordinate with your layout.

Paper edge: Corkscrew by Fiskars

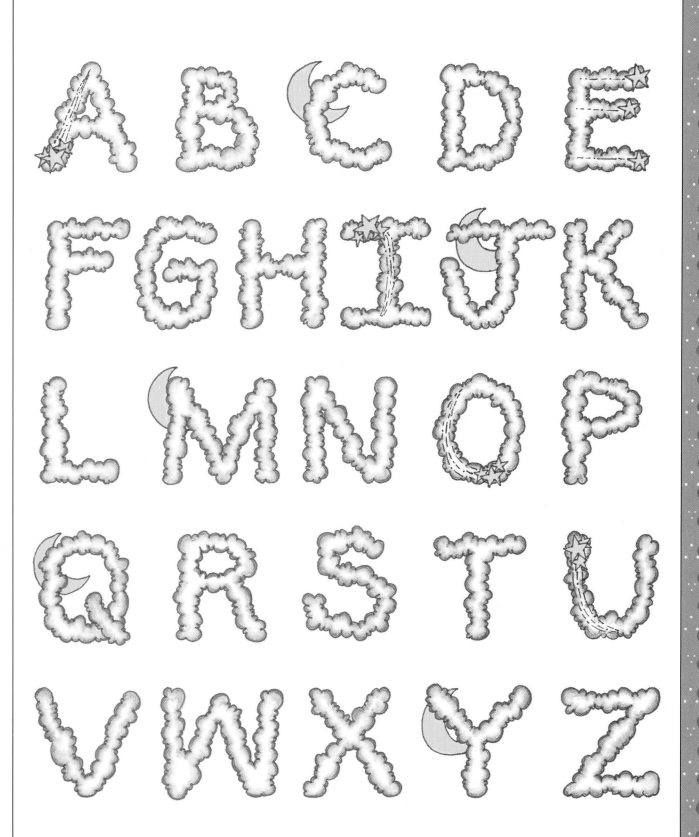

Figure 2. The Sweet Dreams Alphabet adds the perfect touch to layouts of your slumbering angel. **Supplies** *Pen:* Zig Writer, EK Success; *Watercolor pencils:* Rexel Derwent.

ters with a marker, then erase the pencil lines. (*Note:* Remember to outline the stars and moons first in case they overlap the letters.)

④ **Color in your title.** When coloring in your letters, don't feel limited to using blue. The Sweet Dreams Alphabet adds a softness that will complement any baby layout (see Figures 3-4). You can add shadows (see the "It's a Girl" example at right) or stitch marks (see the "Sweet Dreams" example at right). The sky's the limit!

Enjoy this sweet little alphabet that can enhance your baby layouts while bringing back the softness of babyhood. Put your little one down for a nap and create titles that'll give *you* sweet dreams! ♥

Figure 3. Shading, stitch marks and shadows are all ways you can vary this alphabet.
Supplies *Pens:* Zig Writer, EK Success; Milky Gel Roller, Pentel; *Patterned paper:* Making Memories ("It's a Girl"); Paperbilities, MPR ("It's a Boy"); PrintWorks ("Sweet Dreams").

Figure 4. For a different look, cut out each letter and create a free-flowing title. Pages by Heather Holdaway Thatcher. **Supplies** *Pens:* Zig Writers, EK Success; *Watercolor pencils:* Rexel Derwent; *Patterned paper:* The Paper Patch; *Patterned vellum:* Sonburn; *Specialty paper:* Sponge paper, Wintech; *Clocks:* Cross My Heart; *Bear:* MM's Design; *Pop dots:* All Night Media; *Lotion, chair, dresser and pacifier:* Heather's own designs. *Idea to note:* This layout highlights Heather's birth and her husband's.

archival angels©
preserve precious memories

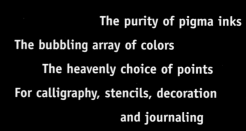

The purity of pigma inks
The bubbling array of colors
The heavenly choice of points
For calligraphy, stencils, decoration
and journaling

illustration
scrapbooking
stenciling
calligraphy
crafts

PIGMA COLOR TECHNOLOGIES

CONFORMS TO
ASTM D-4236

ideal for
acid free
environments

water proof
ph neutral
fade proof
archival permanent

pigma micron, pigma callipen, pigma brush & pigma graphic

power to express™

Oh, Baby!

She is growing and changing every day, right before your eyes.

Savor the moment, the celebration, the everyday triumphs that touch your family's life.

Scrapbooking is a direct reflection of your love and caring spirit—just like the superior quality of the unique products we design and create.

Hold on to her a little longer by capturing the memory with Current.

Caitlin Mellisa September 14th

BABY

Current®

WAITING FOR BABY

You were a good baby before you were even born. I had a really good pregnancy—Thanks!

August 19

March

Just starting to show.

Look whos tired.

"Weight'ing FOR YOU"

Belly battling with Rondi Lance.

large

April *May* *June*

Baby's kickin'!

July

medium

October *November*

August *Sept*

October 25

Big as a PUMPKIN!

October 23 *November 23*

December

PHOTO TIP:

Just because baby's not here doesn't mean there aren't photos to be taken. You may want to capture some of these moments on film:

- Mom's growing belly
- Filling out adoption paperwork
- Preparing the nursery
- The completed nursery
- Shopping for baby clothes, crib, stroller and other items
- Baby showers

"Weight'-ing for You"
by Heidi Allen
Everett, Washington
SUPPLIES

Scissors: Clouds edge, Fiskars
Lettering template: Ol' Calhoon, D.O.T.S.
Pens: Milky Gel Roller, Pentel; Zig Writer, EK Success; Crystal Point, Marvy Uchida
Computer font: Curlz, Microsoft Word
Calendars: Microsoft Works
Shirts: Heidi's own designs

"Peek-a-Boo . . . We See You"

by Heidi Allen

Everett, Washington

SUPPLIES

Patterned paper: Northern Spy

Lettering template: Ol' Calhoon, D.O.T.S.

Scissors: Maxi Zig-Zag edge, Making Memories; Pinking and Deckle edges, Fiskars

Stethoscope die cut: Ellison

Pens: Crystal Point and Artist, Marvy Uchida

Colored pencils: Prismacolor, Sanford

Bear clip art: Dazzle Daze, D.J. Inkers

Other: Heidi included an Anne Geddes greeting card on the layout.

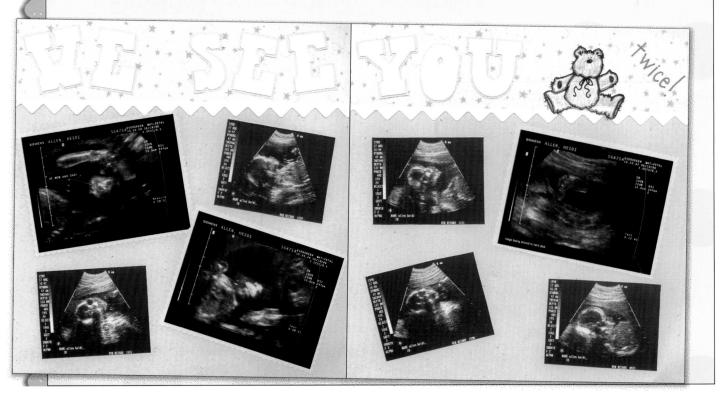

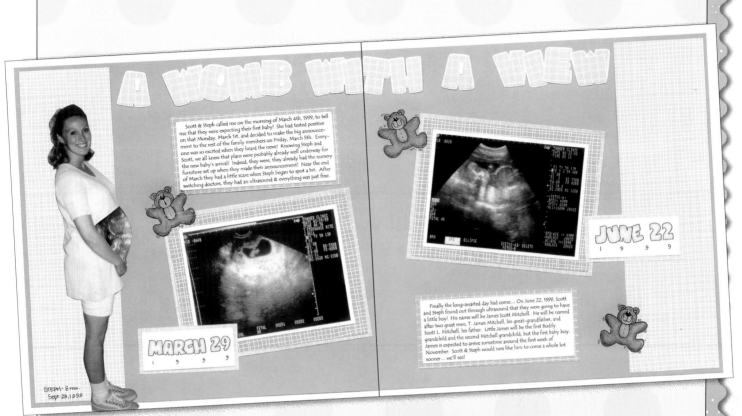

Scott & Steph called me on the morning of March 4th, 1999, to tell me that they were expecting their first baby! She had tested positive on that Monday, March 1st, and decided to make the big announcement to the rest of the family members on Friday, March 5th. Everyone was so excited when they heard the news! Knowing Steph and Scott, we all knew that plans were probably already well underway for the new baby's arrival! Indeed, they were, they already had the nursery furniture set up when they made their announcement! Near the end of March they had a little scare when Steph began to spot a bit. After switching doctors, they had an ultrasound & everything was just fine.

MARCH 29 1 9 9 9

JUNE 22 1 9 9 9

Finally the long-awaited day had come... On June 22, 1999, Scott and Steph found out through ultrasound that they were going to have a little boy! His name will be James Scott Mitchell. He will be named after two great men, T. James Mitchell, his great-grandfather, and Scott L. Mitchell, his father. Little James will be the first Bodily grandchild and the second Mitchell grandchild, but the first baby boy. James is expected to arrive sometime around the first week of November. Scott & Steph would sure like him to come a whole lot sooner... we'll see!

STEPH+ 8 mos. Sept. 23, 1999

"A Womb with a View"

by Brenda Bennett
Morenci, Arizona

SUPPLIES

Patterned paper: Close To My Heart/D.O.T.S.
Rub-on transfers: Provo Craft
Lettering template: Fat Caps, Frances Meyer

Computer font: Tempus Sans ITC, Microsoft Word
Colored pencils: Prismacolor, Sanford
Pen: Zig Writer, EK Success
Idea to note: Brenda scanned the ultrasound images and printed them so she could manipulate their sizes.

JOURNALING IDEA:

Whether you're pregnant or waiting for the adoption notification, try to keep a daily journal. Record feelings, emotions, hopes for your baby and the progression of the adoption or pregnancy. If you journal on loose paper, you can simply slip the entries into the baby's scrapbook or use snippets from your journal as your photo journaling. (A daily journal is especially important for adoptive parents—this way you can tell your child what you were doing on his or her birthday.)

Paper edge: Corkscrew by Fiskars; Die cut: Pebbles in my Pocket; Die-cut art by Kristy Banks of Highland, UT

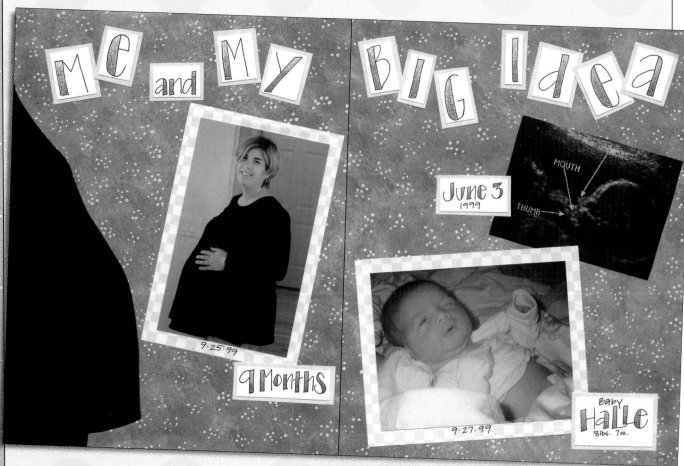

ME and MY BIG Idea

June 3
1999

MOUTH
NOSE
THUMB

9·25·99

9 Months

9·27·99

Baby
Halle
8lbs. 7oz.

"Me and My Big Idea"

by Kristina Nicolai-White
Two Peas in a Bucket
Middleton, Wisconsin

SUPPLIES

Patterned paper: Provo Craft (speckled);
The Paper Patch (checked)
Colored pencils: Memory Pencils, EK Success
Pens: Gelly Roll, Sakura; Zig Writer, EK Success
Memorabilia idea: Include ultrasound and
electrocardiogram strips in your scrapbook.
Also include copies of any prescriptions or
advice your doctor gives you.

THAT'S OUR BOY

THE LIL' GUYS PROFILE.

HE'S FLEXING HIS ARM!

DEC.'97
John & I Went in for our
ultrasound and ... ITS A BOY!
Daddy can hardly wait to
teach his son SOCCER, and
lots of other stuff! Yippee!!!

"That's Our Boy"

by Brooke McLay
Colorado Springs, Colorado
SUPPLIES

Patterned paper (large soccer balls):
Frances Meyer
Soccer-ball stickers: Sandylion
Pens: Zig Millennium, EK Success;
Milky Gel Roller, Pentel

"Sweet Dreams"
by Marilyn Healey
West Jordan, Utah
SUPPLIES
Patterned paper: Frances Meyer
Punches: Marvy Uchida (small star); McGill (medium and large star)
Lettering template: Block Serif, Pebble Tracers, Pebbles in my Pocket
Chalk: Craf-T Products
Ink pad: Stampin' Up!
Pens: Micron Pigma, Sakura; Artist, Marvy Uchida
Moon: Marilyn's own design
Other: Marilyn used embroidery floss on her layout.
Idea to note: Marilyn got the idea for the baby from a Stampin' Up! stamp.

"You've Got the Cutest Little Baby Face"
by Annabeth Goss
West Jordan, Utah
SUPPLIES
Lettering template: Dot, Pebble Tracers, Pebbles in my Pocket
Pen: Zig Writer, EK Success

Idea to note: Annabeth used a silhouette technique to trace the profile of her and her husband, then included the profiles on her layout.

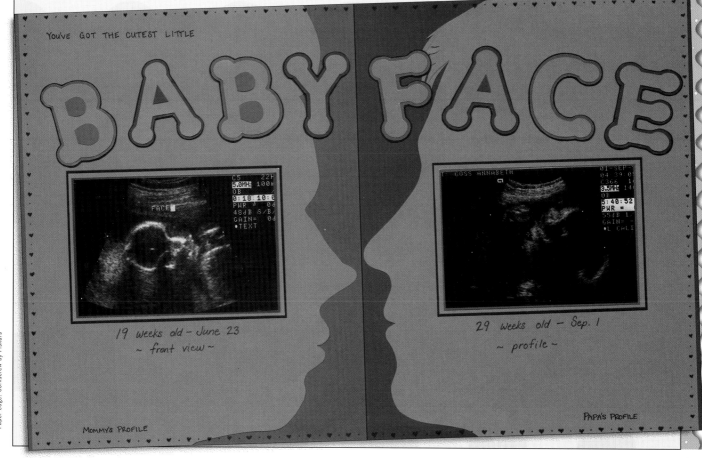

Paper edge: Corkscrew by Fiskars

"These Gals from Ricks Are Now Raising Chicks"

by Heidi Allen
Everett, Washington
SUPPLIES
Patterned paper: The Paper Patch
Chick stickers: Mrs. Grossman's
Chick template: Happy Everything, Provo Craft
Pens: Zig Writer, EK Success; Crystal Point, Marvy Uchida
Computer fonts: CK Fill In and CK Script, "The Best of Creative Lettering" CD Vol. 1, *Creating Keepsakes*
Nest, barn, fence and "YOU": Heidi's own designs

"Baby Shower"

by Brenda Bennett
Morenci, Arizona
SUPPLIES
Patterned paper: Close To My Heart/D.O.T.S.
Specialty paper: The Paper Company (vellum paper)
Baby clip art: Dazzle Daze, D.J. Inkers
Computer font: CK Script, "The Best of Creative Lettering" CD Vol. 1, *Creating Keepsakes*
Lettering template (date): Fat Caps, Frances Meyer
Colored pencils: Prismacolor, Sanford
Chalk: Craf-T Products
Title: Brenda's own design

"Baby Shower"

We were lucky enough to have two baby showers. Janice and Mary hosted the first one and Sandy hosted the second one. We played silly games, opened gifts and ate lots of cake. We received so many wonderful gifts from everyone.

"Baby Shower"

by Kim Heffington
Puzzle Mates
Brea, California

S U P P L I E S

Umbrella template: Rainy Day, Puzzle Mates
Patterned paper: Sonburn
Gift die cuts: Stamping Station
Punches: All Night Media (spiral); Family Treasures
(daisy); Marvy Uchida (sun)
Hole punches: Punchline, McGill
Computer fonts: CK Anything Goes and CK Print,
"The Best of Creative Lettering" CD Vol. 1, *Creating Keepsakes*
Colored pencils: Prismacolor, Sanford

My Mom gave me one of my baby showers in her backyard. It was done beautiful - great food and fun games. My Dad picked out the cake from Kings Hawaiian bakery - Yum! We had a great day with about 50 friends ☺ 8-16-97

me & my Mom and baby still in my tummy. This is the cake that my Dad had made especially for me at Kings Hawaiian bread in Torrance, California

baby got so-o many gifts that it took 2 trips in my Cherokee and an extra trip with the mini-van to get home!

"Baby Shower"

by Sonya Wilkinson-Wyeth
Lansing, Michigan

S U P P L I E S

Patterned paper: Keeping Memories Alive
Page title: Page Toppers,
Cock-A-Doodle Design, Inc.
Punches: All Night Media (spiral, flower); McGill (bow)
Pen: Zig Writer, EK Success
Gifts: Sonya's own designs

JOURNALING IDEA:

In your scrapbook, include short personal histories of the baby's parents, grandparents and even great-grandparents. Be sure to include photos and handwriting samples along with the histories. (This is a great complement to a family tree layout.) If a personal history is too daunting a task, ask the baby's grandparents to write letters to the baby and include those in the scrapbook.

Paper edge: Corkscrew by Fiskars; Die cut: Pebbles in my Pocket; Die-cut art by Kristy Banks of Highland, UT

BABY QUILT

GRANDMA LAURSEN

As soon as Grandma Laursen found out mommy was pregnant, she immediately started to sew a baby quilt for her future first grandbaby. She finished this quilt in under one month and mailed it to mommy! Mommy loved it and knew her new baby would love all the animals on it. And guess what? He did! Austin loved to lay on his tummy and stare at all the different animals and colors. He is three years old now and still sleeps with his special baby quilt.

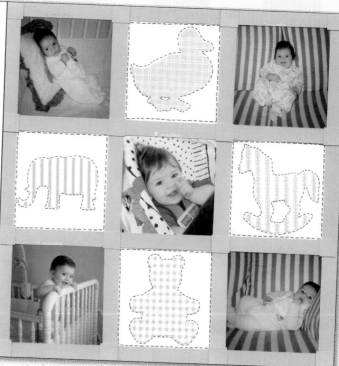

"Baby Quilt"

by Tracy Managan
Pittsburg, California

SUPPLIES

Lettering template: Fat Caps, Frances Meyer
Patterned paper: The Paper Patch (striped and gingham); Northern Spy (plaid)
Computer font: DJ Squared, Fontastic!, D.J. Inkers
Pen: Zig Writer, EK Success

"Dress Up"

by Marilyn Healey
West Jordan, Utah

SUPPLIES

Patterned paper: Colors By Design
Lettering template: Classic, Pebble Tracers, Pebbles in my Pocket
Scissors: Scallop edge, Fiskars
Pen: Zig Millennium, EK Success
Chalk: Craf-T Products

Baby doll: Marilyn's own design
Other: Marilyn used muslin and ribbon on the layout.
Photo op: Take photos of the clothes or gifts you received at baby showers and include the photos in your scrapbook. These photos will serve as great reminders of friends and their generosity.

Dress Up

These are just a few of the clothes that Grandma Leffler and Aunt Lea sent.

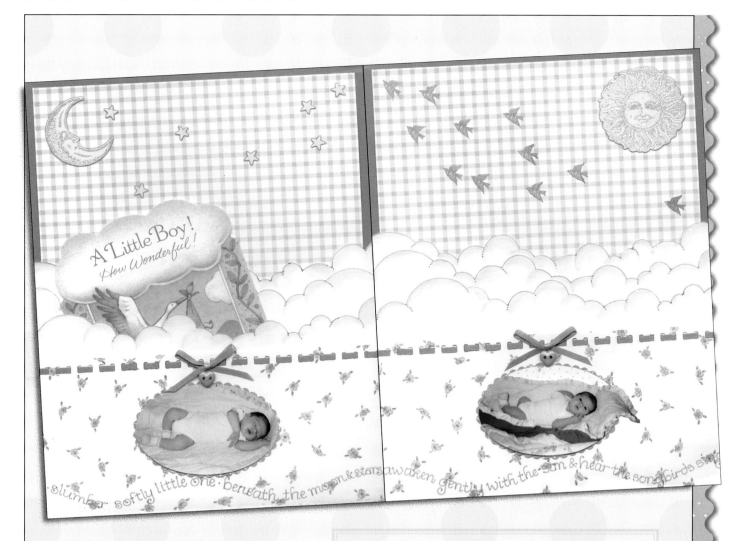

Paper edge: Corkscrew by Fiskars; Die-cut: Pebbles in my Pocket; Die-cut art by Kristy Banks of Highland, UT.

"Slumber Softly Pocket Page"

by Genevieve Glassy
Tenino, Washington

SUPPLIES

Patterned paper: NRN Designs (flowers); The Paper Patch (plaid)

Rubber stamps: Rubber Stamps of America (moon, sun); Sweet Impressions (bird)

Star punch: McGill

Scissors: Scallop edge, Fiskars

Pens: Tombow; Gel Pen, Marvy Uchida

Clouds: Genevieve's own design

Idea to note: Genevieve included ribbon and buttons on her layout.

Memorabilia Idea:

Congratulatory cards you receive at showers and following your baby's birth are terrific items to include since they contain hand-written thoughts and signatures from your friends and loved ones. You may also want to ask family members to write notes to the baby. Just be sure to test the acid content of the cards and letters and deacidify them if necessary. (Note: If you receive flowers after you give birth, consider pressing them and including some flowers in your scrapbook along with the cards.)

"My Room"
by Ellen James
Orem, Utah
S U P P L I E S

Lettering template: Classic, Pebble
Tracers, Pebbles in my Pocket
Computer font: Tempus Sans, WordPerfect
Idea to note: Ellen used the fabric from the
room as her patterned paper.

"London's Noah's Ark Nursery"
by Marilyn Healey
West Jordan, Utah
S U P P L I E S

Patterned paper: The Paper Patch
(blue-and-white gingham); Keeping Memories Alive
(yellow-and-white plaid); Close To My Heart/D.O.T.S.
(pink-and-white plaid)
Lettering template: Classic, Pebble Tracers,
Pebbles in my Pocket
Chalk: Craf-T Products
Pen: Micron Pigma, Sakura
Ark, animals and hearts: Marilyn's own designs

My Mom wanted my room to be perfect
for my arrival, so she started remodeling
months before. First my Mom, Aunt
Jennifer and Grandma Cozzens all helped
paint my room lemon white. Then my Dad
painted my ceiling sky blue. Lisa Jimenez,
one of my Mom's friends, painted clouds
and stars on my ceiling and a quote that
she repeated around the room, "Babies are
bits of stardust blown from the hand of
God." My Mom & Dad put up a cute
border and my Mom picked out this fabric
from a design book. Charlene Berhand, a
friend from the ward, made the bedding
and curtains for my room.

"Preparing the Ark"

by Heidi Allen

Everett, Washington

SUPPLIES

Patterned paper: Keeping Memories Alive

Noah stationery: Rebecca Carter, Provo Craft

Letter stickers: Country Alphabet and Noah's Journey,
Debbie Mumm, Creative Imaginations

Pen: Zig Millennium, EK Success

Paper edge: Corkscrew by Fiskars; Punch art created by Scrapbook Haven in Portland, OR.

Memorabilia Idea:

Adding swatches of nursery-room fabric and

wallpaper is a great way to bring back memories.

You may even want to include swatches of fabric

from your child's favorite blanket or from his or

her christening outfit. (Note: Some wallpaper is

made of vinyl. If your wallpaper swatch is made

from vinyl, simply color-copy it and include the

color copy in your scrapbook.)

"Labor of Love"

by Cynthia Castelluccio
Carrollton, Virginia

SUPPLIES

Lettering template: Fat Caps, Frances Meyer
Photo frame and stickers: Boyds Bears,
InterArt Dist./Sunrise
Daisy punch: Family Treasures
Pen: Le Plume II, Marvy Uchida
Hearts: Cynthia's own designs
Idea to note: Cynthia used raffia
to make borders on the layout.

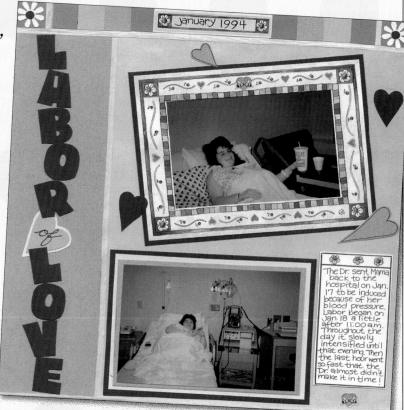

PHOTO TIP:

Now that baby's almost here, be sure
to capture some of these "must-have"
moments on film:

- First family photo of mom,
  dad and newborn baby
- Newborn baby in mom's arms
- Newborn baby in dad's arms
- Baby being held by siblings
- Baby with grandparents and
  other relatives
- Baby with family pets

"New Year's False Alarm"

by Cynthia Castelluccio
Carrollton, Virginia

SUPPLIES

Patterned paper: Provo Craft
Circle punches: Family Treasures
Lettering template: Rounded, Pebble Tracers,
Pebbles in my Pocket
Hat and mitten die cuts: Creative Memories
Computer font: DJ FiddleSticks Bold,
Inspirations, D.J. Inkers
Scissors: Deckle edge, Fiskars
Pens: Zig Writer, EK Success;
Precious Element, Creative Memories
Snowballs, baby and alarm clock: Cynthia's own designs

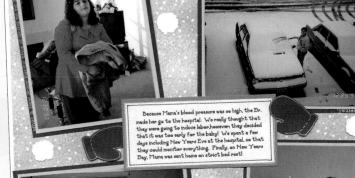

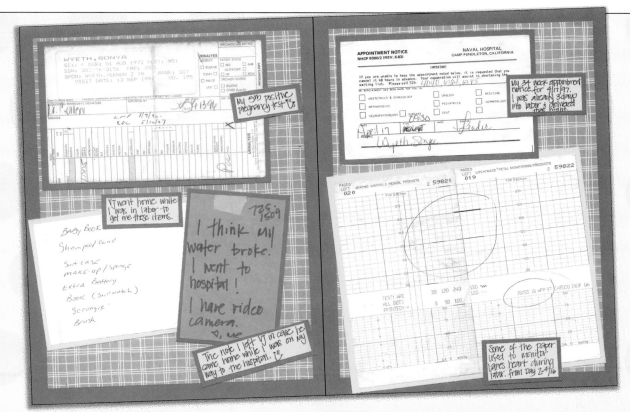

"Labor Memorabilia"

by Sonya Wilkinson-Wyeth
Lansing, Michigan

SUPPLIES

Patterned paper: Northern Spy
Pen: Zig Writer, EK Success

"What's in a Name?"

by Merrilynne Harrington
Springville, Utah

SUPPLIES

Patterned paper: Colors By Design
Stickers: me & my BIG ideas
Lettering template: Block, Pebble
Tracers, Pebbles in my Pocket
Pen: Zig Writer, EK Success

Ideas to note: Merrilynne made her own background paper by writing out the baby names she and her husband were considering. She mounted the translucent stickers on white cardstock before putting them on her layout.

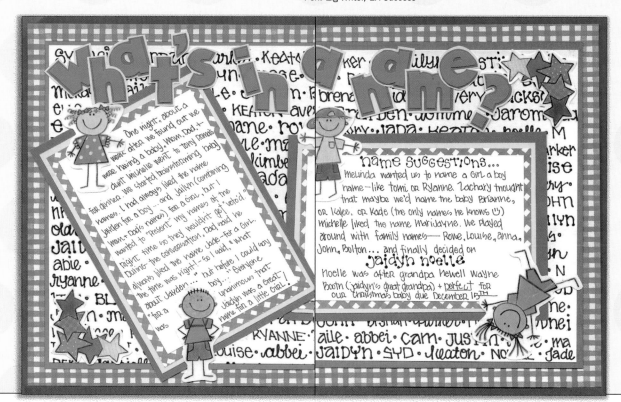

How we picked your name:

Daisy: *This is your great-grandmother's name (MiMi's mom). I chose this name for you because I've always loved and admired my Nana. I hope that you will share in some of her characteristics. She is a beautiful woman, a dedicated Christian, a hard worker and the best cook I've ever known! Daisy means 'eye of the day' and 'cheerful.'*

Rebecca: *This is after your MiMi (Erin's mom). Rigdon and I decided that I could choose the name of a girl baby and he'd pick if you had been a boy. I chose my mom's name for you because she is a wonderfully sweet woman who would do anything for her family. She is a good Christian and is always kind to others. Rebecca is a biblical name meaning 'to bind' and 'beautiful.'*

"How We Picked Your Name"

by Erin Terrell
San Antonio, Texas

SUPPLIES

Specialty papers: Paper Adventures (suede paper for leaves); Personal Stamp Exchange (mulberry paper)
Leaf template: Provo Craft
Hole punch: Punchline, McGill
Chalk: Derwent
Pen: Artist, Marvy Uchida

Computer font: Nuptual, Microsoft Word
Journaling idea: If you named your child after a family member or close friend, be sure to include the significance of the name, any special memories of the person your baby's named after, and even the etymological roots of the name.

"Looks Like a Legacy"

by Michelle Gowan
Macon, Georgia

SUPPLIES

Patterned paper: The Paper Patch (plaid); Frances Meyer (stars)
Stickers: Frances Meyer
Photo-tinting pens: SpotPen
Computer font: DJ Dash, Fontastic!, D.J. Inkers
Layout idea: Make a generational layout showing traits or similarities from one generation to the next. Combining heritage photos with current ones is a terrific way to connect the generations.

Looks Like a Legacy

Charles Gregg Gowan 1941

David Charles Gowan 1965

Charles Gregg Gowan II 1998

63 *Terrific Titles to Pamper Your Layout*

N ow that you've captured your sweet little one on film, it's time to put those photos in your scrapbook. If you're stumped trying to find the perfect title or phrase to capture your little one's first year, check out these cuddly titles. They're sure to deliver bundles of smiles!

BEFORE THE BABY'S BIRTH

✳ "Full Disclosure" .... Telling your family that you're expecting

✳ "Our Love 'Abounds'," "Growing by Leaps and Bounds," "We're Building a Family" .... Your month-to-month growth

✳ "Pickles, Anyone?" .... Recording your cravings

✳ "Great Expectations" .... Your hopes and dreams for your baby

✳ "A Womb with a View," "A Sneak Peek" .... Your ultrasound photos

✳ "What's up, Doc?" .... Your visits to the obstetrician

✳ "The Perfect Place" .... The baby's nursery

✳ "Showered with Love" .... Your baby showers

✳ "A Labor of Love" .... Your labor

DURING THE BABY'S FIRST DAYS

✳ "Give That Man a Cigar" .... The proud father

✳ "On the Day You Were Born" .... Historical statistics

✳ "Your New Home" .... Your baby's first home

✳ "The Grand Entrance" .... Arriving home

✳ "And Baby Makes Three," "Then There Were Three" .... The new family

✳ "Hand in Hand" .... The baby's small hand in a parent's large hand

✳ "10 Tiny Fingers and Toes" .... Close-up photos of baby's hands and feet

✳ "Bridging the Generation Gap" .... The first time meeting grandparents

✳ "Meet Our New Arrival" .... The first time meeting friends

✳ "It's All Relative" .... The first time meeting relatives

✳ "Sibling Rivalry" .... Sibling's reactions to the new arrival

✳ "Family Ties" .... The family portrait

✳ "A Proud Proclamation," "Meet Our Newest Addition," "The New Kid on the Block" .... Baby's birth announcement

✳ "A Blessed Day" .... Baby's christening

Paper edge: Corkscrew by Fiskars; Die cuts: Ellison (buttons); Pebbles in my Pocket (pacifier, rattle); Die-cut art by Kristy Banks of Highland, UT

DURING THE BABY'S FIRST YEAR

* "My Big Adventure" . . . . Baby's first outing
* "On a Roll" . . . . Baby rolls over
* "Sitting Pretty" . . . . Baby sits up
* "Look What Just Popped Up" . . . . Baby's first tooth
* "Moving at a Snail's Pace" . . . . Baby crawls
* "Upwardly Mobile" . . . . Baby pulls self up
* "Something's Afoot," "The Pitter-Patter of Little Feet" . . . . Baby walks
* "Grin and Bear It" . . . . Baby smiles
* "A 'Hair-Raising' Experience" . . . . Baby's first haircut
* "A Feast Fit for a King" . . . . Baby eats
* "Our 'Bubbly' Baby," "Rub-a-Dub-Dub," "Bathing Beauty," "The Bare Necessities"
. . . . Baby in the bath
* "Dream Big," "Hush Little Baby," "Lullaby and Goodnight," "Beautiful Dreamer,"
"Sweet Dreams," "Catching Some ZZZZ's" . . . . Baby sleeping

GENERIC TITLES FOR GIRL LAYOUTS

"I Feel Pretty, Oh So Pretty"

"Sugar and Spice"

"Drop-dead Gorgeous"

"My Heart Belongs to Daddy"

"Daddy's Girl"

GENERIC TITLES FOR BOY LAYOUTS

"Boy Wonder"

"Big Boy"

"Boys Will Be Boys"

"Our Little Tyke"

GENERIC TITLES

"Innocent Until Proven Guilty"

"Caught Red-Handed"

"You've Got the Cutest Little Baby . Face"

"It's a 'One'-derful Day"

"I'm 'Two'-riffic"

QUOTABLE QUOTES

If a title doesn't express just the right sentiment, check out these sayings.
They're sure to add a fun dimension to any layout.

Monday's child is fair of face,
Tuesday's child is full of grace,
Wednesday's child is full of woe,
Thursday's child has far to go,
Friday's child is loving and giving,
Saturday's child works hard
for a living,
And the child that is born
on the Sabbath day
Is bonny and blithe, and good
and gay.
—*Traditional poem*

People always ask what
am I going to be
when I grow
up and I always
just think
I'd like to grow
up
—*Nikki Giovanni*

♥

Never forget for a single minute,
You didn't grow under my heart,
But in it.
—*Unknown*

And all my toys beside me lay
To keep me happy all the day. . . .
—*Robert Louis Stevenson*

♥

I have a little shadow that goes in
and out with me,
And what can be the use of him is
more than I can see. . . .
—*Robert Louis Stevenson*

♥

Golden slumbers kiss your eyes,
Smiles awake you when you rise. . . .
—*Thomas Dekker*

If you were the kid, we'd be the candy store.

PageToppers, Vols 1–4!

Beautiful, easy-to-use, hand-rendered designs that measure 8.5" by 2.75"— perfect for use on either standard or 12" by 12" pages. Acid-free, lignin-free cover stock to last through the generations. Purchase separately or in 40-piece value paks. *The perfect way to "top off" that perfect page!*

PagePrintables CD!

Print illustrated page titles directly from your computer to your printer! Includes 60 new PageToppers, 10 colorized alphabets and 15 lettering/journaling fonts. *The perfect way to "print" that perfect page!*

PagePocket Guide!

This convenient, 32 page full-color booklet shows you how to use all of our fantastic products to create your own perfect scrapbook pages. Tons of great page layout and theme ideas. *The perfect way to "develop" that perfect page!*

PagePieces!

Designed to coordinate perfectly with Pagetoppers to create a professional, finished touch to your scrapbook pages! Each strip has 3 die-cut illustrations held in place by a few microscopic tufts of paper. They're beautifully printed and so easy to tear out without damage. *The perfect way to "finish off" that perfect page!*

We give you something to crow about!

Call **1-800-262-9727** to order, or to find a retailer in your area!
Or visit our website at **www.cockadoodledesign.com**

Cock-A-Doodle Design, Inc.
801-954-0554   fax 801-954-0564

MY FIRST YEAR

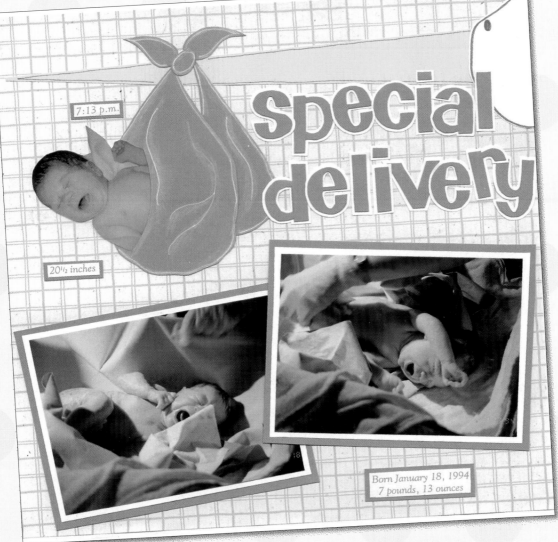

7:13 p.m.

20½ inches

special delivery

Born January 18, 1994
7 pounds, 13 ounces

"Special Delivery"
by Cynthia Castelluccio
Carrollton, Virginia
SUPPLIES
Patterned paper: Over The Moon Press
Pens: Le Plume, Marvy Uchida;
Milky Gel Roller, Pentel
Colored pencils: Memory Pencils, EK Success
Lettering template: Classic, Pebble Tracers,
Pebbles in my Pocket
Stork and wrap: Cynthia's own designs

JOURNALING IDEA:

*Don't forget to include this
information in your scrapbook:
Date of delivery
Duration of delivery
Name and location of hospital
Name of doctor
Names of attending nurses*

"The World When You Were Born"

by Merrilynne Harrington
Springville, Utah
S U P P L I E S
Patterned paper (on pants): Colors By Design
Specialty paper: Sandylion (sparkle paper);
Therm O Web (foam paper); Accu-Cut Systems
(metallic paper)
Punches: Family Treasures (spiral); McGill
(star, flower); Marvy Uchida (triangle)
Hole punch: Punchline, McGill
Note die cut: Ellison
Pen: Zig Writer, EK Success

Lettering template: Block,
Pebble Tracers, Pebbles in my Pocket
Cup, world, CD and clothes:
Merrilynne's own designs
Journaling idea: Give historical perspective to
your baby's birth date by recording the cost
of everyday items, such as a gallon of milk,
a gallon of gasoline and a loaf of bread. You
may also want to include the highlights of the
year, such as governmental figures, World
Series winners and other pop-culture items.

"Michael Jessie Wheeler"

by Tamara Wheeler
Hurricane, Utah
S U P P L I E S
Patterned paper: Northern Spy
Lettering template: Block,
Pebble Tracers, Pebbles in my Pocket
Stickers: Suzy's Zoo
Page title: Page Toppers,
Cock-A-Doodle Design, Inc.
Memorabilia pocket: 3L Corp.

Paper edge: Corkscrew by Fiskars

"It's a Boy"
by Cynthia Castelluccio
Carrollton, Virginia
SUPPLIES
Patterned paper: Michel & Company
Stationery: Michel & Company
Pen: Le Plume II, Marvy Uchida
Computer font: Kidprint, downloaded from *www.netpedia.com*
Lettering template: Fat Caps, Frances Meyer
Idea to note: Cynthia included her son's birth announcement on the layout.

"Love at First Sight"
by Carol Banks
Newhall, California
SUPPLIES
Patterned paper: Provo Craft
Alphabet letters: Alphabitties,

Repositionable Sticky Die-Cut
Letters, Provo Craft
Heart punches: Marvy Uchida
(medium); Family Treasures (large)
Pen: Zig Writer, EK Success

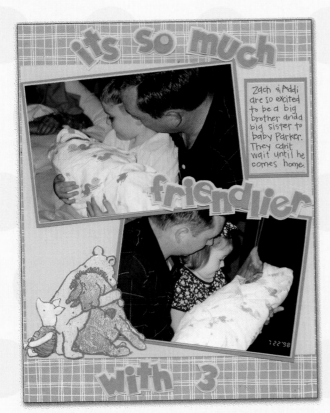

"It's So Much Friendlier with 3"
by Jennifer Jensen
Hurricane, Utah
SUPPLIES
Patterned paper: Northern Spy
Winnie the Pooh die cuts: Michel & Company
Pen: Zig Writer, EK Success
Lettering template: Block, Pebble Tracers, Pebbles in my Pocket

It's a Girl!

Here, Terry and Dennis (a.k.a. Mom and Dad T.) visit with Daisy the day after she was born. They came to help us out around the house and help get Daisy's room set up. She was born earlier than expected. I was planning on having a whole extra week or two to prepare for a baby! They were a big help in taking care of the house, buying diapers, washing baby clothes, etc. I think they got kind of bored after 5 days in the hospital, though! Dad T. saw it as a good time to catch up on his naps!

And she's absolutely beautiful! Daisy Rebecca Terrell Born November 12, 1997 at 4:24 P.M. Weighing in at 5 lbs. 14 oz. and 21 inches long.

Rigdon and I have been waiting forever for this day!! Until now, we thought we were having a boy. We even told a few people we thought we were having a boy. That's because of something my doctor once told me. I reminded her (Dr. Vora) every time I had a sonogram that I didn't want to know whether the baby was a boy or a girl. She was pretty good and never told me, until one day. I hadn't reminded her because I wasn't having a sonogram, just a normal check-up. She asked, "Do you know if you're having a boy or a girl?". I said, "No". Then, before I could tell her that I didn't want to know, she blurted out, "It's a boy! I can tell by the heartbeat!". Argghh! I was so mad! Then, after a second, I was happy to know and I went home and told Rigdon. We let a lot of people know we thought it would be a boy, but BOY were we wrong! It was a happy surprise! When Daisy was born and Dr. Vora said, "It's a girl!" I looked at Rigdon and said, "Is that OK?" He just laughed at me and said, "What if it isn't? Are you going to put her back?" (Funny guy I married, huh?!) I think I may have even asked the doctor if she was sure it was a girl! I remember hearing Daisy cry and cry. Right after she was first born, the doctor put her on my tummy for me to hold. Soon afterwards, they whisked her away for a good cleanup and thorough exam (which she passed with flying colors! Her bilirubin count was low, but that was about the only problem.) Rigdon got busy making phone calls to tell the family of our big news. Mom and Dad Terrell already knew I was in labor and

had started the 5 hour drive up from San Antonio. They arrived just a couple hours after Daisy was born. They couldn't believe she came so fast, but delivery is usually faster when someone is induced and when they don't have an epidural (which I didn't). Mom and Dad Wactor had been talking to Rigdon on the phone off and on during my labor. They were so excited to hear that we had a little girl and that we named her 'Daisy', after my mom's mom, and 'Rebecca', after my mom. My mom had no idea that we were going to do that, so it was a nice surprise.

I did have some complications during the pregnancy. My labor was induced on the 12th of November (Daisy's original due date was the 20th) because I had to be admitted to the ER the night before for severe back pains.

I had preeclampsia, PIH (Pregnancy Induced Hypertension) and HELLP syndrome (Hemolysis; Elevated Liver function tests; and Low Platelets). It was all very scary for me and a typical ending for a very stressful pregnancy! Luckily, our skilled doctor brought Daisy and I through the delivery very well and we ended up weak, but fared much better than many women and babies who contract HELLP syndrome.

"It's a Girl"

by **Erin Terrell**
San Antonio, Texas

SUPPLIES

Patterned paper: Keeping Memories Alive (plaid); The Paper Patch (flower)
Heart punch: Marvy Uchida
Pens: Zig Writer, EK Success; Milky Gel Roller, Pentel
Colored pencils: Prismacolor, Sanford
Lettering templates: Scrapbook, Provo Craft; Block Serif, Pebble Tracers, Pebbles in my Pocket
Specialty paper: Personal Stamp Exchange (mulberry paper)
Idea to note: Erin got the idea for the baby from a Leow Cornell sticker.

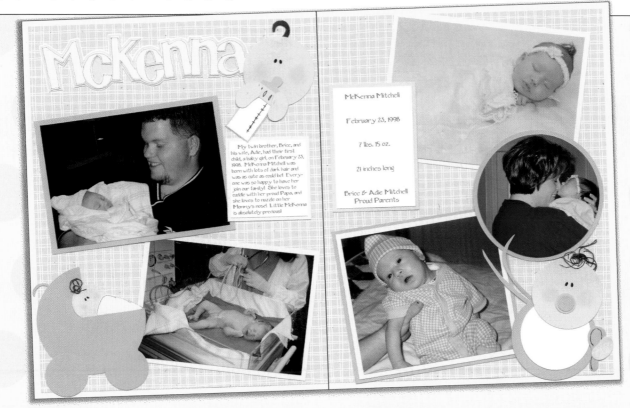

McKenna Mitchell

February 23, 1998

7 lbs. 15 oz.

21 inches long

Brice & Adie Mitchell
Proud Parents

My twin brother, Brice, and his wife, Adie, had their first child, a baby girl, on February 23, 1998. McKenna Mitchell was born with lots of dark hair and was as cute as could be! Everyone was so happy to have her join our family! She loves to cuddle with her proud Papa, and she loves to nuzzle on her Mommy's nose! Little McKenna is absolutely precious!

Paper edge: Corkscrew by Fiskars

"McKenna"

by Brenda Bennett
Morenci, Arizona
S U P P L I E S

Patterned paper: Northern Spy
Punches: Marvy Uchida (small circle); Family Treasures (medium circle); All Night Media (spiral)
Pen: Zig Writer, EK Success

Computer font: DJ Classic, Fontastic!, D.J. Inkers
Lettering template: Classic, Pebble Tracers, Pebbles in my Pocket
Chalks: Craf-T Products
Babies, bottle, spoon, bib, carriage and pacifier: Brenda's own designs

"My First Day"

by Debbie Singson
Orem, Utah
S U P P L I E S

Patterned paper: Provo Craft
Punches: Marvy Uchida (bear, butterfly); Family Treasures (tulip, rabbit)
Die cuts: Pebbles in my Pocket

Computer font: Scrap Simple, Lettering Delights Vol. 2, Inspire Graphics
Page title: Page Toppers, Cock-A-Doodle Design, Inc.
Idea to note: Debbie laced twine throughout the layout.

Kayley Nicole

April 7, 1999
11:29 a.m.

my first day

7 lbs 7 oz
18-1/2 inches

Kayley

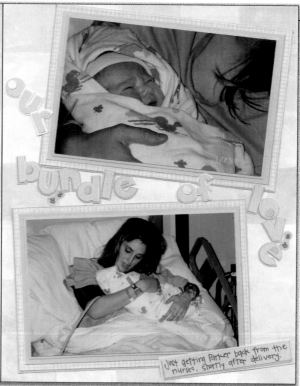

What a special day.. our new baby boy is finally here- he is so beautiful and perfect. we are so blessed to have you little Parker. We love you little one.

July 21, 1998

Just getting Parker back from the nurses, shortly after delivery.

"Sent from Above, Our Bundle of Love"

by Jennifer Jensen
Hurricane, Utah

SUPPLIES

Patterned paper: Keeping Memories Alive (plaid); Michel & Company (Winnie the Pooh, pastel background)

Bee stickers: Michel & Company

Pen: Zig Writer, EK Success

Lettering template: Block, Pebble Tracers, Pebbles in my Pocket

"Hospital Visitors"

by Ellen James
Orem, Utah

SUPPLIES

Patterned paper: Paper Adventures

Letter die cuts: Ellison

Feet die cuts: Accu-Cut Systems

Pen: Zig Writer, EK Success

my sister Janissa

my brother Andrew

Jennifer was so excited

aunt Karen

aunt Leslie

aunt Jennifer, Devon & Logan

aunt Karen, Marianne, Lisa & Kimberly

PHOTO TIP:

Don't forget to include photos of the important people in your baby's life. Here are a few suggestions:

- Parents
- Grandparents
- Siblings
- Aunts and uncles
- Cousins
- Playmates
- Baby–sitters
- Obstetrician
- Pediatrician

"Zachary Hiram Glenn"
by Karen Glenn
Orem, Utah
SUPPLIES
Hole punches: Punchline, McGill
Pen: Zig Writer, EK Success
Blocks and corner enhancements:
Karen's own designs
Idea to note: Karen added
silk ribbon to the layout.

"First Photos"
by Brenda Bennett
Morenci, Arizona
SUPPLIES
Patterned paper: Close To My Heart/D.O.T.S.
Stickers: Paper House Productions
Pen: Hybrid Gel Roller, Pentel
Colored pencils: Prismacolor, Sanford
Photo corners: Canson

The angels knew mommy needed a good baby. That's why they sent her ME! I am so happy and I sleep like a log. Mommy loves me so much.
2 1/2 weeks old

"Heaven Sent"
by Kristy Banks
Highland, Utah
S U P P L I E S
Patterned paper: Northern Spy
Clip art: Zip Art, Special Effects Illustration, Inc.
Computer fonts: CK Simplicity and CK Toggle, "The Best of Creative Lettering" CD Vol. 2, *Creating Keepsakes*
Die cuts: Ellison
Chalk: Craf-T Products

"Special Delivery"
by Gayle Holdman
American Fork, Utah
S U P P L I E S
Rubber stamps: D.O.T.S.
Ink pads: Marvy Matchable, Marvy Uchida
Pens: Le Plume II, Marvy Uchida;

My Legacy Writer, D.O.T.S.
Scissors: Mini-Scallop edge, Fiskars
Journaling idea: Consider writing down your feelings, thoughts, hopes and dreams for your little one and including them on a layout.

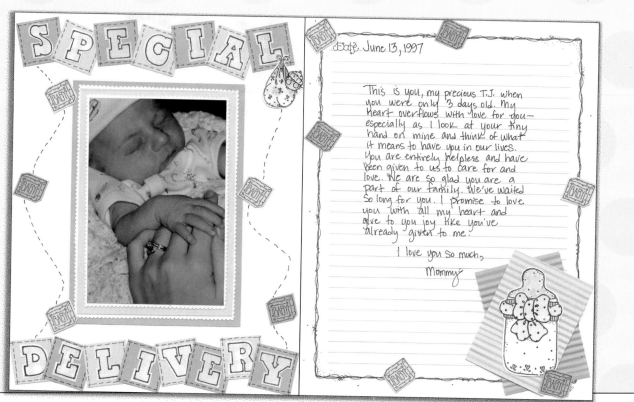

Date June 13, 1997

This is you, my precious T.J. when you were only 3 days old. My heart overflows with love for you—especially as I look at your tiny hand on mine and think of what it means to have you in our lives. You are entirely helpless and have been given to us to care for and love. We are so glad you are a part of our family. We've waited so long for you. I promise to love you with all my heart and give to you joy like you've already given to me.

I love you so much,

Mommy

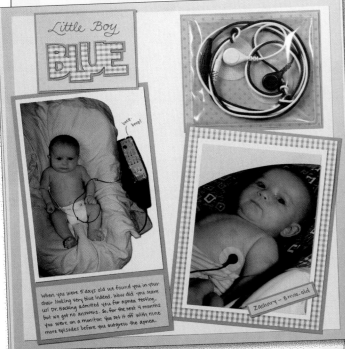

"Little Boy Blue"

by Karen Glenn
Orem, Utah

SUPPLIES

Patterned paper: The Paper Patch
Specialty paper: Paper Adventures (patterned vellum)
Pen: Zig Writer, EK Success
Memorabilia pocket: 3L Corp.
Title: Karen's own design
Memorabilia idea: Karen included her son's monitor cords on the layout.

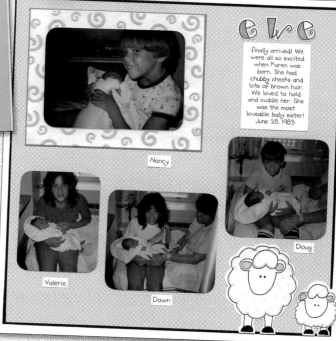

"Ewe Finally Arrived"

by Nancy Church
Augusta, Georgia

SUPPLIES

Patterned paper: The Paper Patch
Specialty paper: Paper Adventures (velveteen paper)
Decorated die cuts: My Mind's Eye
Punches: Family Treasures (spiral); All Night Media (mini-spiral)
Pen: Platinum Writer, EK Success
Computer fonts: CK Anything Goes and CK Toggle, "The Best of Creative Lettering" CD Vol. 1 and Vol. 2, *Creating Keepsakes*
Tool tip: Nancy used the Xyron machine to adhere the velveteen paper.

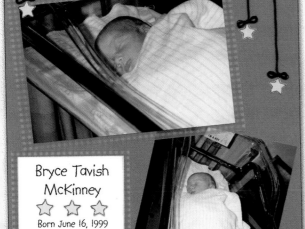

"A Blessing from Heaven"

by Carol Banks
Newhall, California

SUPPLIES

Page title: Page Toppers, Cock-A-Doodle Design, Inc.
Star punch: McGill
Specialty paper: Making Memories (printed vellum)
Computer font: Kidprint Regular, downloaded from *www.netpedia.com*
Pen: Zig Writer, EK Success
Idea to note: Carol "hung" the stars with embroidery floss.

"Korbin's Blessing Day"
by Brenée Williams
Boise, Idaho

SUPPLIES

Computer font: Source unknown, Microsoft Word

Memorabilia idea: Consider including baby booties, hair ribbons and color copies of your baby's christening outfit in your scrapbook. These tactile items will bring back memories of how small your baby once was.

"Bless the Little Ones"
by Heidi Allen
Everett, Washington

SUPPLIES

Specialty paper: Paper Adventures (printed vellum); Frances Meyer (embossed paper)

Stationery: Frances Meyer

Scissors: Seagull and Stamp edges, Fiskars

Pens: Zig Writer, EK Success; Hybrid Gel Roller, Pentel

Computer font: DJ Script Bold, Dazzle Daze, D.J. Inkers

Alphabet rubber stamps: D.O.T.S.

Idea to note: Heidi included her daughter's headband on the layout.

Memorabilia idea: Include copies of the birth certificate, hospital bill, card from the adoption agency and other paperwork in your scrapbook. (Remember that original documents should always be stored in a safe or a fireproof box.)

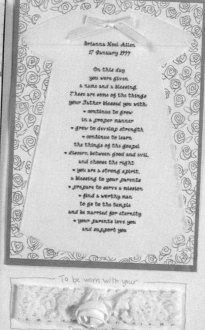

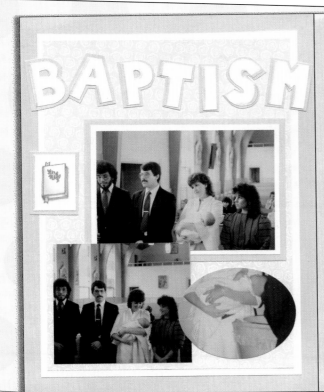

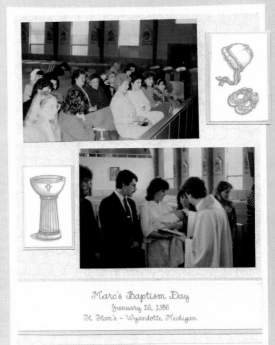

Marc's Baptism Day
January 26, 1986
St. Stan's ~ Wyandotte, Michigan

A Name and a
Blessing

— *August 1, 1999* —

Zachary Hiram Glenn

"Baptism"
by Pam Talluto
Rochester Hills, Michigan
SUPPLIES
Patterned paper: The Paper Patch
Stickers: Frances Meyer
Pen: Tombow
Computer font: DJ Fancy, Fontastic!, D.J. Inkers
Lettering template: Block, Pebble Tracers,
Pebbles in my Pocket
Idea to note: Pam used a light gray
marker to shade her title.

JOURNALING IDEA:

*Don't forget to write down
the names of people who
attended any baby showers
or christenings.*

"A Name and a Blessing"
by Karen Glenn
Orem, Utah
SUPPLIES
Rectangle punch: McGill
Pen: Zig Calligraphy, EK Success
Idea to note: Karen matted her son's photo on a
swatch of fabric used to create her son's outfit.

July 4 · 1999

This was such a special day for us... our little angel baby was being blessed. We had lots of family & friends come to see you. Daddy gave you a beautiful blessing. He loves his little sweetheart.

The Priesthood bearers who were in the circle
Uncle Josh
Grant Greene
Uncle Jason
Grandpa Hicks
Daddy
Grandpa Dohrman
Grandpa
Uncle Duane
Uncle Ben
Uncle Jonathan and
Uncle Mike

Grandma made your beautiful dress ♡

"Your Blessing Day"

by Jennifer McLaughlin
Back Door Friends—
The Scrapbooking Company
Whittier, California

SUPPLIES

Patterned paper: Mary Engelbreit, InterArt Dist./Sunrise
Pen: Zig Writer, EK Success
Colored pencils: Prismacolor, Sanford
Lettering idea: "Gala" from *The Art of Creative Lettering* by Creating Keepsakes Books
Heart: Jennifer's own design
Idea to note: Jennifer tied an organza ribbon around the page to create a soft look.

"Our Child of God"

by Alycia Alvarez
Altus, Oklahoma

SUPPLIES

Computer font: Pinafore, Create-A-Card
Scissors: Victorian edge, Fiskars
Hole punch: Punchline, McGill
Stickers: The Gifted Line, Michel & Company
Cross die cut: Ellison
Patterned paper: Paper Pizazz, Hot Off The Press

Our Child Of God

Blessings on the little children.
Sweet and fresh from Heaven above.
May their days be filled with beauty.
May they grow in truth and love.
Lord, bless this tiny infant
Who will make the world so fair.
Keep this precious little life
Forever in Your care.

Family is another name for Love

When Brian + I brought Quin home from the hospital the kids were excited and so proud of thier new sister! Tory (9) kept looking for where "the noise" was coming from and Danielle (8) and Alix (7) were thrilled to share thier room with her. Kaed (5) was impressed that he was now a "big brother" and Michael (8) kept saying what a "little angel" Quin was! I love our loving family!!

06/06/98

Paper edge: Corkscrew by Fiskars

"Family Is Another Name for Love"
by Heather Lancaster
Calgary, Alberta, Canada
SUPPLIES
Pens: Zig Writers, EK Success
Hole punch (to thread raffia): Punchline, McGill
Raffia: Plaid
Photo op: Don't forget to take photos of your baby meeting his or her siblings.

"Love, Family, Home"
by Jennifer Jensen
Hurricane, Utah
SUPPLIES
Patterned paper: The Paper Patch
Border, frame and saying: Mary Engelbreit, InterArt Dist./Sunrise
Photo corners: Canson
Pen: Zig Writer, EK Success

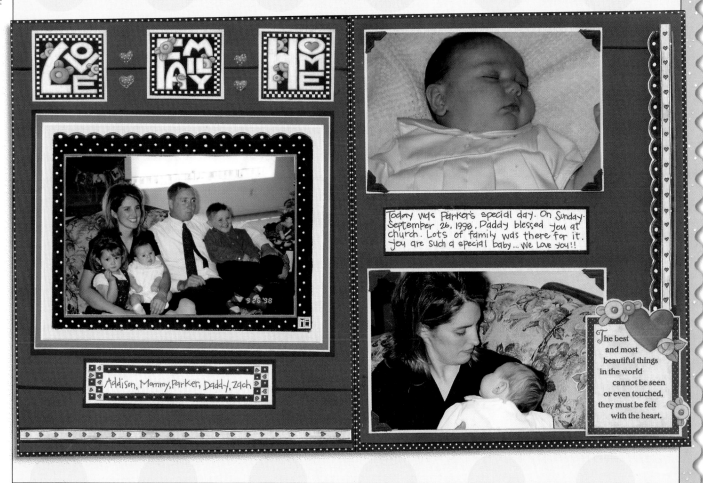

LOVE FAMILY HOME

Addison, Mommy, Parker, Daddy, Zach

Today was Parker's special day. On Sunday. September 26, 1998, Daddy blessed you at church. Lots of family was there for it. You are such a special baby... We love you!!

The best and most beautiful things in the world cannot be seen or even touched, they must be felt with the heart.

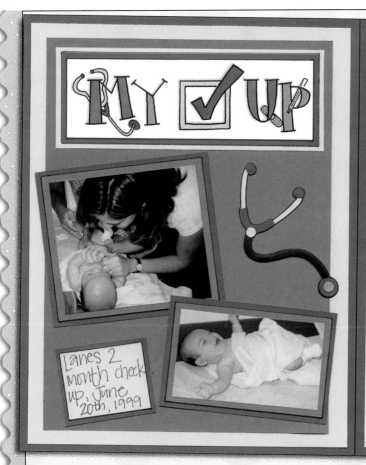

My ☑ Up

Lanes 2
month check.
up, June
20th, 1999

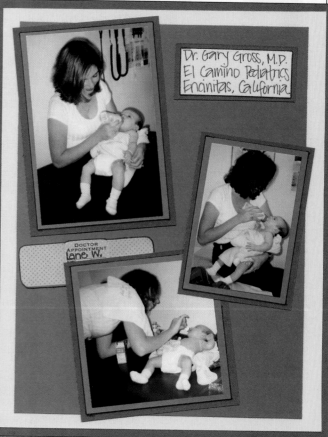

Dr. Gary Gross, M.D.
El Camino Pediatrics
Encinitas, California

DOCTOR
APPOINTMENT
Lane W.

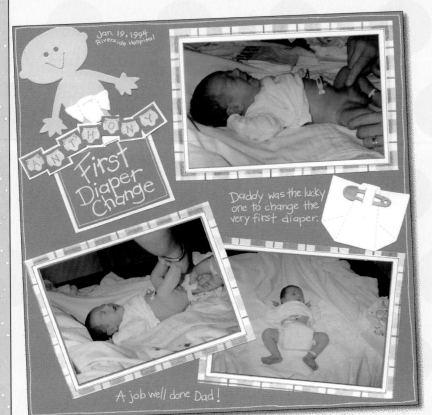

Jan. 19, 1994
Riverside Hospital

ANTHONY

First
Diaper
Change

Daddy was the lucky
one to change the
very first diaper.

A job well done Dad!

"My Checkup"
by Sonya Wilkinson-Wyeth
Lansing, Michigan

SUPPLIES

Page title: Page Toppers,
Cock-A-Doodle Design, Inc.
Die cut: Ellison
Pen: Zig Writer, EK Success
Hole punch: Punchline, McGill
Circle punch: Family Treasures
Bandage: Appointment card from
the doctor

"First Diaper Change"
by Cynthia Castelluccio
Carrollton, Virginia

SUPPLIES

Patterned paper: Paperbilities, MPR
Die cuts: Stamping Station (stick people);
Ellison (diaper, pin)
Diaper letter stickers: Stickopotamus
Pens: Le Plume II, Marvy Uchida;
Milky Gel Roller, Pentel

Daisy's first bath!

She luvs the tub!

Daisy loved her first bath! It's a good thing she isn't shy-Mommy, Daddy, MiMi, Pop Pop and Uncle Craig were all there to witness it! She looked so cute splashing all about! If she takes after her daddy at all, she will definitely be the biggest water baby in town. He was practically a fish growing up! As much fun as Daisy had in the tub, I'm pretty sure she'll turn out the same way!

"Daisy's First Bath"
by Erin Terrell
San Antonio, Texas
SUPPLIES
Patterned paper: Sonburn
Die cuts: Pebbles in my Pocket
Splash template: Funky Shapes, Provo Craft
Letter stickers: Frances Meyer
Pen: Zig Writer, EK Success
Computer font: DJ FiddleSticks,
FiddleSticks, D.J. Inkers
Eye (on duck): Plaid

"First Bath"
by Cynthia Castelluccio
Carrollton, Virginia
SUPPLIES
Patterned paper: The Paper Patch
Circle punch: Family Treasures
Bubble die cuts: Source unknown
Pens: Zig Writer, EK Success; Milky Gel Roller, Pentel
Colored pencils: Memory Pencils, EK Success
Lettering template: Fat Caps, Frances Meyer
Shampoo, soap and duck towel: Cynthia's own designs
Memorabilia idea: Cynthia included her son's washcloth on the layout.

Paper edge: Corkscrew by Fiskars

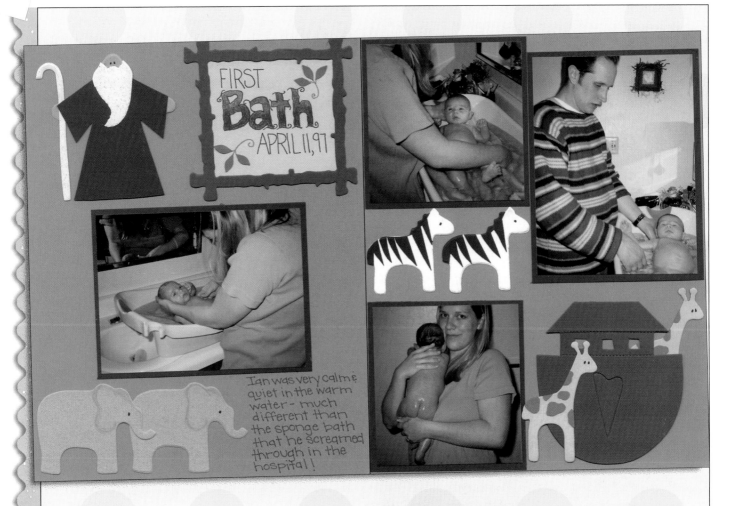

FIRST
Bath
APRIL 11, 97

Ian was very calm & quiet in the warm water - much different than the sponge bath that he screamed through in the hospital!

"First Bath"
by Shannon Wolz
Salt Lake City, Utah
SUPPLIES
Die cuts: The Heartland Paper Co.
Pens: Zig Writers, EK Success
Colored pencils: Prismacolor, Sanford
Lettering idea: "Crooked Classic" from
The Art of Creative Lettering by
Creating Keepsakes Books

"My Favorites"
by Vicki Garner
Windows of Time
Hooper, Utah
SUPPLIES
Paper-piecing pattern:
Little Picasso, Windows of Time
Spoon die cut: Ellison
Pen: Zig Writer, EK Success
Chalk: Craf-T Products
Journaling idea: Don't forget to
record your child's favorite foods.

MY FAVORITES
Bananas
Carrots

Sophia
May 1998
7 months

"Little. Miss Independent"

Fia loves noodles ... especially because she can eat them all by herself!

She eats them by the handfuls... laughing and giggling and slurping and then banging her hand on her tray for more!!

ENJOYING MY VERY FIRST
POPSICLE

ELIZABETH OLSON
JUNE '99

"Little Miss Independent"
by Shauna Dunn
Springville, Utah
SUPPLIES
Pen: Micron Pigma, Sakura
Rotary blade: Wave edge, Fiskars
Fork die cut: Ellison
Pasta: Idea from *Memory Makers* magazine

"First Popsicle"
by Jodi Olson
Redmond, Washington
SUPPLIES
Pen: Zig Writer, EK Success
Colored pencils: Prismacolor, Sanford
Drop template: Funky Shapes, Provo Craft
Popsicle lettering: Jodi's own design

We skipped the baby food & went right to the good stuff. You ate rice cereal maybe five times & then wouldn't have anything to do with it. Your all-time favorites were cheerios, blueberry bagels, graham crackers, noodles, rice, cheese, apple juice, breastmilk (of course), & anything Mom & Dad were eating.

PRIZES
1. "Held the longest interest in". The pickle made a great teether.
2. "Most likely to get Mom in a tizzy!" That's what grandparents are for. P.S.—that's Mom's old dentist watching my daughter eat wedding cake!
3. "Most likely to cause Mom to do some laundry". What a mess!

LOVE at first bite

Chowin' on rice cereal!

Can we eat now!

Silver Spoon Awards

"Silver Spoon Awards"

by Heidi Allen
Everett, Washington
S U P P L I E S

Patterned paper: Close To My Heart (circles);
Northern Spy (plaid); Frances Meyer (border)
Spoon die cut: Ellison
Alphabet letters: Fat Dots,
Repositionable Sticky Die-Cut Letters, Provo Craft
Pens: Zig Fine & Chisel, EK Success;
Crystal Point, Marvy Uchida
Ribbon template: School, Pebble Tracers,
Pebbles in my Pocket
Idea to note: Heidi added a ribbon to each spoon.

YUM YUM PABLUM!

♥ PABLUM EATING TIPS ♥   02/10/93
1- CHECK LABELS FOR YUCKY STUFF
2- APPROACH WITH CAUTION
3- BE PREPARED TO EXPEL & REJECT
4- REMEMBER, IT CAN ONLY GET BETTER!

"Yum, Yum—Pablum!"

by Heather Lancaster
Scrapbooker's Paradise
Calgary, Alberta, Canada
S U P P L I E S

Patterned paper: NRN Designs
Letter stickers: Frances Meyer
Rabbit stickers: Source unknown

JOURNALING IDEAS:

Important Dates and Firsts to Record:

- First bath
- First smile
- Rolling over
- Sitting up
- Laughing
- Up on all fours

- Crawling
- Pulling self up
- Reaching for an object (tell what it was)
- Getting first tooth

- Standing on own
- First step
- Walking
- Saying first word (tell what it was)
- Tasting new foods

- First haircut
- First visit to Santa
- First holidays
- First illness

Daisy took her first steps in September of 1998 when she was almost 10 months old. She was so cute trying to keep her balance! The first time she actually walked on her own was in October when we were on our trip to SC. She walked back and forth between Rigdon and her Uncle Craig. Pop Pop videotaped the whole thing! Everyone would clap for each step she took and she loved all of the attention!

"First Steps"

by Erin Terrell
San Antonio, Texas
SUPPLIES

Patterned paper: Keeping Memories Alive
Letter stickers: Sticky Sentiments, It Takes Two
Border stickers: me & my BIG ideas
Colored pencils: Prismacolor, Sanford
Computer font: DJ FiddleSticks, FiddleSticks, D.J. Inkers
Template: Provo Craft

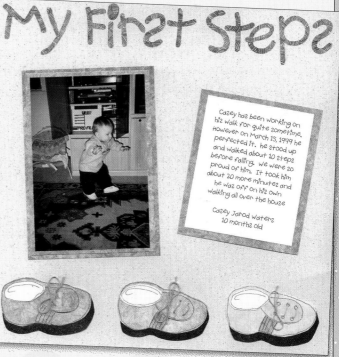

Casey has been working on his walk for quite sometime. However on March 15, 1999 he perfected it. he stood up and walked about 10 steps before falling. we were so proud of him. It took him about 20 more minutes and he was off on his own walking all over the house

Casey Jarod Waters
10 months old

"My First Steps"

by Emily Waters
Provo Craft
Provo, Utah
SUPPLIES

Patterned paper: Provo Craft
Computer font: Scrap Kids, Lettering Delights Vol. 2, Inspire Graphics
Shoe clip art: Just for Fun, D.J. Inkers

Paper edge: Corkscrew by Fiskars

"Oh, The Things You Say"

by Brooke McLay
Colorado Springs, Colorado

SUPPLIES

Pens: Zig Writer, EK Success; Hybrid Gel Roller, Pentel
Colored pencils: Memory Pencils, EK Success
Patterned paper: D.J. Inkers
Stickers: Frances Meyer (hot dog, doughnut, candy corns); Mrs. Grossman's (stars); Stickopotamus (hand); Sandylion (basketball)

"Famous First Words"

by Heather Holdaway Thatcher
Draper, Utah

SUPPLIES

Patterned paper: Keeping Memories Alive
Pens: Zig Writers and Zig Opaque Writers, EK Success; Tombow
Blocks: Heather's own designs
Lettering idea: CK Baby Bottle, "The Best of Creative Lettering" CD Vol. 1, *Creating Keepsakes*
Idea to note: This layout shows both Heather's first word and her husband's.

JOURNALING IDEA:

Be sure to record these items:
Your child's first words and phrases
Cute things your child says
Funny ways your child pronounces words

Paper-piecing pattern: Windows of Time; Paper-piecing art by Windows of Time in Hooper, UT

Quin started talking at about eight months old. Her first official word according to Mom was 'up', but Dad insists it was 'dad' (of course!). At eleven months old Quin now says hi, dad, up, dog dog, nigh nigh (her blanket), all done and an occasional mom mom. Quin also makes very specific, very funny noises for the word juice and cookie!

May '99

"Quin's First Words"
by Heather Lancaster
Scrapbooker's Paradise
Calgary, Alberta, Canada
S U P P L I E S
Patterned paper: Keeping Memories Alive (maroon plaid); Paperbilities, MPR (pink plaid)
Pen: Zig Writer, EK Success
Photo corners: Canson
Raffia: Plaid
Envelopes: Heather's own designs

"Oh No!"
by Amy Williams
Ogden, Utah
S U P P L I E S
Patterned paper: Over The Moon Press (flower); Keeping Memories Alive (speckled)
Pen: Le Plume, Marvy Uchida
Computer font: Delano, Corel Draw
Lettering templates: Puffy and Alphabet Soup, Provo Craft
Dress and shoes: Amy's own designs

OH NO!

One thing we love about Marinne is her independence. One day while trying to get her ready she says, "I do it my bigself." I think it was harder than she expected. Her dress ended up inside out and it became a skirt. The shoes of choice were actually mommies and they were two different pair, but at least they were both brown. Later she finished the job off with one grey mitten and a baseball cap.

Marinne, 20 months old. May 1999

My First Home

I arrived at my first home at 5111 Daffodil Way San Jose CA on February 14, 1974

"My First Home"
by Emily Waters
Provo Craft
Provo, Utah
S U P P L I E S
Patterned paper: Provo Craft
Computer font: Scrap Simple, Lettering Delights Vol. 2, Inspire Graphics
Alphabet letters: Kids, Repositionable Sticky Die-Cut Letters, Provo Craft
Brick rub-on transfers: Provo Craft

Paper edge: Corkscrew by Fiskars

Brynne's Little Baby

milestones

June 3rd – 1 month old

your first smile was at about 10 days old... but this is the first picture we have of your beautiful smile!

You started "cooing" at about 4-5 weeks old
you squealed with delight on June 19th
your first laugh was on August 24th
during the week of July 5th you discovered your hands
On Aug. 18th you discovered your feet

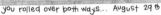

You picked up an object...

July 29th

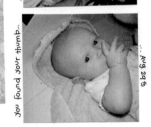

You found your thumb...

Aug 29th

you rolled over both ways... August 29th

...Little baby milestones....

....there's a first time for everything....

...watching you experience these simple joys....

....makes our hearts sing!

"Milestones"

by Jennifer McLaughlin
Back Door Friends—The Scrapbooking Company
Whittier, California
SUPPLIES
Patterned paper: Provo Craft (grass, speckled); Source unknown (flowers)
Stickers: Paper House Productions
Pen: Zig Writer, EK Success
Lettering template: Classic, Pebble Tracers, Pebbles in my Pocket
Stones and grass: Jennifer's own designs

"Some Firsts"

by Ellen James
Orem, Utah
SUPPLIES
Patterned paper: Northern Spy
Stickers: Creative Memories
Pen: Zig Writer, EK Success

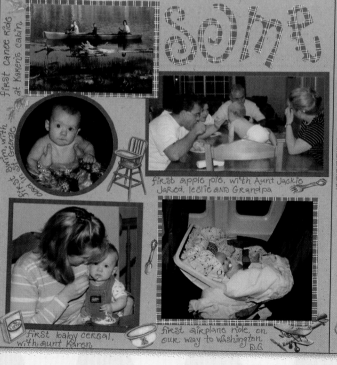

some firsts

First canoe ride at Karen's cabin

first swim, with my pop at St. George

first apple pie, with Aunt Jackie, Jared, leslie and Grandpa

first baby cereal, with aunt Karen

first airplane ride, on our way to Washington D.C.

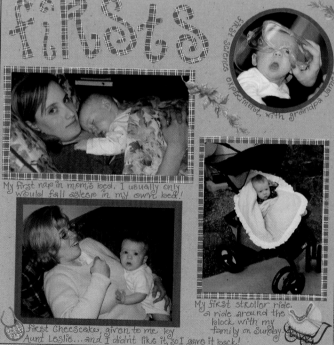

first science experiment, with grandpa James

My first nap in mom's bed. I usually only would fall asleep in my own bed!

first cheesecake, given to me by Aunt Leslie...and I didn't like it, so I gave it back!

My first stroller ride, a ride around the block with my family on Sunday

---

136   Creating Keepsakes • My First Year

"My Artwork"
by Pam Talluto
Rochester Hills, Michigan
SUPPLIES
Patterned paper: NRN Designs
Star punches: Family Treasures
Pen: Zig Writer, EK Success
Page title: Page Toppers,
Cock-A-Doodle Design, Inc.
Decorated die cuts: Page Pieces,
Cock-A-Doodle Design, Inc.

"Fia-Fang"
by Shauna Dunn
Springville, Utah
SUPPLIES
Patterned paper: The Paper Patch
Die cuts: Pebbles in my Pocket
Stickers: Stickopotamus
Lettering template: Rounded Serif, Pebble
Tracers, Pebbles in my Pocket
Pens: Zig Writer and
Zig Opaque Writer, EK Success

Paper edge: Corkscrew by Fiskars

"Proof of a Tooth"

by Heidi Allen
Everett, Washington

SUPPLIES

Patterned paper: The Paper Patch
Scissors (on brush bristles): Deckle edge, Fiskars
Tooth die cut: Ellison
Pens: Zig Calligraphy, EK Success; Crystal Point, Marvy Uchida
Lettering template: Block Serif, Pebble Tracers, Pebbles in my Pocket
Journaling tooth: PrintMaster, Mindscape
Paper crimper (on brush bristles): Fiskars
Toothbrush and tooth chart: Heidi got the idea for these items from a Carnation direct-mail piece.

"First Tooth"

by Nancy Church
Augusta, Georgia

SUPPLIES

Patterned paper: Keeping Memories Alive
Hole punches: Punchline, McGill
Punches: Family Treasures (circle); All Night Media (mini-spiral)
Rub-on transfers (eyes): Provo Craft
Pen: Zig Millennium, EK Success
Computer font: DJ Crayon, Fontastic!, D.J. Inkers
Lettering template: Block, Pebble Tracers, Pebbles in my Pocket
Chalk: Stamping Station
Hair, bows and teeth: Nancy's own designs

my First Haircut

September 1, 1999

On a spur of the moment idea, we met Dad at his appointment at Pat's Cut & Curl. Debbie agreed to give Austin a trim. Your hair was past your eyebrows & over your ears! Attached below is <u>all</u> of the hair she trimmed off!

Snip, Snip, Snip!

...After

Memorabilia Idea:

Don't forget to keep a lock of your baby's hair from his or her first haircut. You can store the hair in one of the many memorabilia pockets available.

"My First Haircut"

by Pamala Gandolfi
Prudenville, Michigan
SUPPLIES
Patterned paper: Provo Craft
Scissors: Deckle edge, Fiskars
Die cut: Accu-Cut Systems
Stickers: Frances Meyer
Pen: Zig Writer, EK Success
Memorabilia pocket: 3L Corp.

"Kayden's First Haircut"

by Marci Leishman
Draper, Utah
SUPPLIES
Computer font: DJ Crazed, Fontastic! 2, D.J. Inkers
Page title: Page Toppers, Cock-A-Doodle Design, Inc.
Memorabilia pocket: 3L Corp.
Circle punch: McGill
Idea to note: Marci included the receipt and card from the barber shop.

KAYDEN'S FIRST haircut

NOVEMBER 12, 1996
18 MONTHS OLD

LIL' Hair Cuts

BEFORE

DURING

AFTER

Kayden wouldn't even sit on the special animal chairs. He insisted on having Mommy hold him. Watching Barney on TV didn't even help! Kayden was sooooo scared of the clippers and cried the whole time! But afterward, Kade looked great! He was even a little proud of his new hair-do.

Kayden was not happy about having his first official haircut (Granny Hunt had trimmed off a few stray hairs a few months before). His hair was growing so slow that we though a trim might help things out a bit. His stylist at the Lil' Things Hair Salon must have thought we were crazy when we brought Kayden in for a haircut! What hair???

Frequent
Hair Cut
Club
LIL' Things
FREE
Name

"Baby Ian's First Year"

by Shannon Wolz
Salt Lake City, Utah

SUPPLIES

Patterned paper: Paper Pizazz, Hot Off
The Press (denim); Frances Meyer (leaf);
Provo Craft (large and small plaid);
Keeping Memories Alive (plaid);
Current, Inc. (flower, gingham)

Pen: Zig Writer, EK Success

Specialty paper: Paper Adventures
(printed vellum)

Idea to note: Shannon "sewed" different
elements to her background paper to
repeat the quilt in the photos.

"Watch Me Grow"
by Yuko Neal
Huntington Beach, California
SUPPLIES
Letter die cuts: Ellison
Stickers: NRN Designs (numbers);
remember when . . ., Colorbök (Bryce & Madeline);
Mrs. Grossman's (trains, toys)
Pen: Zig Clean Color, EK Success

"Watch Me Grow"
by Marilyn Healey
West Jordan, Utah
SUPPLIES
Pen: Micron Pigma, Sakura
Lettering template: Funky, Pebble Tracers,
Pebbles in my Pocket
Scissors: Deckle edge, Fiskars
Hearts: Marilyn's own designs

watch me **GROW**

each picture was taken on the 24th of each month.

7 months

8 months

9 months

10 months

11 months

Happy Birthday!! taken at 9:26 a.m.

12 months

13 months

1 year old !! on Friday October 24, 1997

from Austin's mommy and Daddy.

from G & G Openshaw →

Austin's Birthday

PRESENTS

from Uncle Wayne, Aunt Jen, Trent & Chris

from Bobby

from G&G Openshaw

We ate at Round Table Pizza with Grandpa & Grandma Healey. We played games at the party and had a fun time.

from Mommy & Daddy (airplane)
from G&G Openshaw (pop-beads)

from G&G Healey

PHOTO TIP:

Is your tyke turning one or entering the "terrible twos"? Don't miss out on these fun birthday photo ops:

- Decorations
- Guests
- Guests interacting with baby
- The birthday cake
- Baby blowing out the candles
- Baby eating the birthday cake
- Baby opening presents (or just playing in the empty boxes!)
- Individual shots of the birthday presents
- Baby surrounded by the gifts
- Baby interacting with the gifts

"Austin's Birthday Presents"

by Marilyn Healey
West Jordan, Utah
SUPPLIES

Scissors: Deckle edge, Fiskars
Pen: Micron Pigma, Sakura
Stickers: Frances Meyer
Journaling idea: Marilyn took photos of her son's birthday presents and included them on the layout. She then listed who each present was from.

Paper edge: Corkscrew by Fiskars; Die cuts: Stamping Station; Die-cut art by Stamping Station in Layton, UT

"Crumbie, Crumbie Birthday!"

by Kimberly Ann Morgan
Pleasant Grove, Utah

SUPPLIES

Patterned paper: The Paper Patch (flower, dark-blue gingham); Close To My Heart/D.O.T.S. (light-blue gingham)
Pen: Callipen, Sakura
Cake: Kimberly's own design

PHOTO TIP:

Parents take a *lot* of photos during baby's first few years. Remember an important rule of scrapbooking—select only the best photos for your scrapbook. This way you won't get overwhelmed with scrapbooking, and it's easier to keep current.

"Sweet Cheeks"
by Beth Wakulsky
Haslett, Michigan

SUPPLIES

Patterned paper: Stampin' Up! (polka dot);
Sonburn (striped)
Lettering template: Block Serif,
Pebble Tracers, Pebbles in my Pocket
Cake template: Pebble Tracers, Pebbles in my Pocket
Punches: Family Treasures (small flower, large and
small apples); All Night Media (spiral, border)
Hole punch: Punchline, McGill
Computer font: DJ Serif, Dazzle Daze, D.J. Inkers
Flowers: Idea from *Punch Your Art Out Vol. 2*
by *Memory Makers* magazine

"Happy Birthday"
by Brenée Williams
Boise, Idaho

SUPPLIES

Rubber stamps: D.O.T.S. (cakes); D.J. Inkers (candle)
Chalk (to color in stamped images): D.O.T.S.
Scissors: Scallop edge, Fiskars
Idea to note: Brenée color-copied a page from
her baby book (which contains her mother's
handwriting) and included it on the layout.

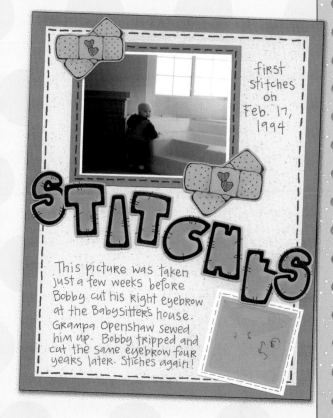

"Ouch!"

by Jana Francis
Provo, Utah

SUPPLIES

Patterned paper: Keeping Memories Alive
Bandage and lettering: Jana's own designs
Pen: Zig Writer, EK Success
Idea to note: Jana tore paper to make
the toilet paper.

Wyatt age 4
he was only still
mad because a
bandaid wouldn't
stick on his lip!!

first
stitches
on
Feb. 17,
1994

STITCHES

This picture was taken
just a few weeks before
Bobby cut his right eyebrow
at the Babysitter's house.
Grampa Openshaw sewed
him up. Bobby tripped and
cut the same eyebrow four
years later. Stiches again!

"Stitches"

by Marilyn Healey
West Jordan, Utah

SUPPLIES

Computer font: DJ Daze, Dazzle Daze, D.J. Inkers
Bandage clip art: Doodlers Vol. 1, D.J. Inkers
Chalk: Craf-T Products
Memorabilia pocket: 3L Corp.
Pens: Micron Pigma, Sakura; Zig Writer, EK Success
Idea to note: Marilyn included some of her son's
stitches on the layout.

Daniel's
first
SPANKING

Daniel got
his first
spanking
for picking
up a book
of matches.
He wanted
a bandaid
to make it
feel better!

"Daniel's First Spanking"

by Debi Boring
Scotts Valley, California

SUPPLIES

Patterned paper:
Keeping Memories Alive (yellow);
Paper Pizazz, Hot Off The Press
(bandage)

Lettering templates: Block Serif,

Pebble Tracers, Pebbles in my
Pocket; Scrapbook, Provo Craft
Large bandage: Enlarged from
patterned paper
Idea to note: Debi scanned and
enlarged the photo to show
Daniel's facial expression.

Paper edge: Corkscrew by Fiskars

by Kristy Banks

Try Our Easy Punch, Sticker and Stationery Borders!

Add a little

sunshine to

your layouts

I F YOU'RE STUMPED FOR THE PERFECT border to enhance your layout, look no further. Here are 12 fun border ideas that'll add the finishing touch to any layout. Whether you've got five minutes or 20, you're sure to find a border that fits your style and time frame!

PUNCHES

There's no doubt about it—punches are a fun and easy way to enhance any layout. And if you're anything like me, you probably have a stash of punches tucked away in your scrapbooking room just begging to be used! So pull out your punches and start creating some of these borders (Figure 1) for your little one!

Before you get started, keep this punching tip in mind: When you punch small items, adhere a photo split or a piece of double-sided tape to the back of your paper *before* you punch out the image. You won't have to worry about trying to put adhesive on those teeny, tiny items.

STICKERS

With the huge variety of stickers available, you're sure to find a sticker for just about any layout theme imaginable (see Figure 2). When making sticker borders, I like to cut the stickers from the sticker sheet first, then arrange them along the

Figure 1. Punched images make perfect borders for any layout. *Borders by Kristy Banks of Highland, Utah ("Bunnies," "Bears and Bottles," Strollers" and "Hey, Diddle Diddle"); Nancy Church of Augusta, Georgia ("Baby Rattles").* **"Bunnies" Supplies** *Patterned paper:* Northern Spy; *Punches:* Family Treasures. **"Bears and Bottles"** *Patterned paper:* Northern Spy; *Punches:* Family Treasures (bottle); Marvy Uchida (bear); All Night Media (Mickey Mouse); *Hole punch:* Punchline, McGill; *Pens:* Zig Writer and Zig Opaque Writer (milk in bottle), EK Success. **"Strollers"** *Punches:* Marvy Uchida (buggy); McGill (heart); *Patterned paper:* The Paper Patch. **"Hey Diddle Diddle"** *Patterned paper:* Keeping Memories Alive; *Punches:* Marvy Uchida (cow and moon); All Night Media (star); *Computer font:* DJ Frilly, Inspirations, D.J. Inkers. **"Baby Rattles"** *Punches:* McGill (circle, star, daisy, small heart); Marvy Uchida (tiny feet, small circle); All Night Media (small flower); *Hole punches:* Punchline, McGill; *Scissors:* Mini-Scallop edge, Fiskars.

Paper edge: Corkscrew by Fiskars

border strip. Once I've arranged the stickers the way I like, I simply remove the paper backing and adhere the stickers to my paper.

When making sticker borders, keep in mind that not all stickers are made the same way. Some stickers have white borders around them, while others don't. Some stickers are even translucent. These traits may determine which background paper you use. If you're using a translucent sticker on a dark background, consider mounting the sticker on white or light-colored paper first. Cut around the sticker, then place it on the dark background paper.

STATIONERY

I'll admit it—every time I visit the scrapbook store, I take a quick trip down the stationery aisle. I love stationery, but sometimes my layouts don't call for a whole sheet of it. My solution? Cut it up and make darling borders like those in Figure 3! I recommend using a craft blade or a pair of fine-tipped scissors to cut out the images. Depending on the background color of the stationery, you may want to cut right along the design's border or, if the background color is neutral, you may want to cut loosely around the edges of the design.

There you have it—three techniques and 12 sample borders that'll help you create great borders without spending a lot of time. With borders this easy, scrapbooking will be child's play! ♥

Figure 2. Stickers are a quick and easy way to make borders. *Borders by Nancy Church of Augusta, Georgia ("Bottles and Booties" and "Let's Eat"); Susan McShirley of S.R.M. Press in Marina del Ray, California ("Baby's Blessing"); Kristy Banks of Highland, Utah ("Bath Time" and "Ribbon and Lace").* **"Bottles and Booties" Supplies** *Stickers:* Frances Meyer; *Patterned paper:* Colors By Design; **"Let's Eat"** *Stickers:* Frances Meyer; *Alphabet letters:* Kid Print, Provo Craft. **"Baby's Blessing"** *Stickers:* S.R.M. Press, Inc.; *Scissors:* Seagull edge, Fiskars. **"Ribbon and Lace"** *Punches:* McGill (bow); Family Treasures (border punch); *Stickers:* me & my BIG ideas. **"Bath Time"** *Patterned paper:* Keeping Memories Alive; *Stickers:* me & my BIG ideas.

Figure 3. Stationery can be cut to create border accents. *Borders by Kristy Banks of Highland, Utah.* **"Baby" Supplies** *Patterned paper:* The Paper Patch; *Stationery:* Suzy's Zoo. **"Baby Clothes"** *Border stickers:* me & my BIG ideas; *Stationery:* Frances Meyer; *Scissors:* Mini-Pinking edge, Fiskars.

Mrs. Grossman's®

A bundle of joy…

Tell your story with a handful of stickers.
Perfect for gifts, announcements, memory books and more.
The possibilities are endless.

*View Mrs. Grossman's newest designs on the Internet at **www.mrsgrossmans.com***
*You'll find lots of sticker art in **Mrs. Grossman's Idea Books®** and **20 Great Ideas™ Books**.*
*Look for them at your favorite sticker store. Call our Consumer Hotline at **1/800-429-4549**. We'd love to hear from you!*

Mrs. Grossman's Paper Company, Box 4467, Petaluma, California 94955

Wholesale Inquiries Only   Ph: (801)444-3828   Fx: (801)444-3827

Sticker Fun for Scrapbooking and More!

Stickers
Sold in rolls or packages
Acid & Lignin Free

Paper Stickers

Prismatic Stickers

Name Stickers

Die Cut Shapes

Sticker Boxes

Scrap Book Stuff

and more...

by Heather Thatcher

Baby your layouts with these titles

D OES YOUR LAYOUT NEED ONE final enhancement? On the next three pages, you'll find a handful of great titles and accents to enhance just about any baby photos you have. Just copy the designs on a copy machine, enlarging or decreasing the size as desired. I recommend copying onto a neutral or light-colored paper, such as white, taupe, cream or gray. This will give you more flexibility when coloring in with pencils, chalks, pens or any other medium you choose. Once your title is colored, simply mat it with cardstock or decorative papers (see Figures 1 and 2). The title will add a finishing touch to your layout! ♥

Figure 1. Enhance a layout with a cute title and frame accents. *Page by Heather Holdaway Thatcher.* **Supplies** *Patterned paper:* Making Memories; *Pen:* Zig Writer, EK Success; *Colored pencils:* Prismacolor, Sanford.

Figure 2. Silhouetting your title adds a unique look to a layout. *Page by Heather Holdaway Thatcher.* **Supplies** *Denim patterned paper:* Paper Pizazz, Hot Off The Press; *Pens:* Zig Writer and Zig Opaque Writer, EK Success; *Carousel:* Heather's own design.

Paper edge: Peaks by Fiskars

Family Ties

Bathing Beauty

Little Tyke

Babies Have More Fun

THE Pitter-Patter OF LITTLE FEET

I'm 2-Riffic

BABY *Shower*

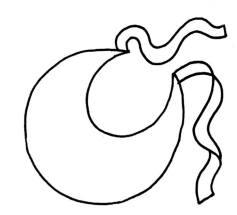

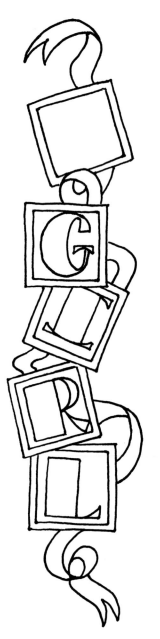

GIRL

B**I**G
THINGS COME IN
LI**T**TLE
PACKAGES

BOYS *WILL BE* BOYS

I love making a
Mess

Lullaby and

GOODNIGHT

Your New Home

Sugar and Spice

New Kid on the Block

HUSH LITTLE BABY

Peek-a-boo

5 Tips for Taking Terrific Photos

Hone your photography skills

A BABY CHANGES SO MUCH IN TWO short years, from being a sleepy, snuggly newborn to being a curious crawler. During this time you'll experience tons of moments you'd no doubt love to capture on film. Read on to learn five basic tips that'll help you improve your photography skills.

❶ Simplify the background. Pay close attention to the background when you're taking a photo. A simple background allows you to focus on your baby. Be sure to change your position until the background is free of distracting items.

❷ Get closer. By getting close to your baby, you're able to capture your baby's priceless expressions. Try to coax your baby to look straight into the camera lens. Many point-and-shoot cameras are now equipped with telephoto lenses. If you have one, use it; if you don't, move several feet forward.

❸ Add variety to your photos. Taking photos from different angles can create some fun results. Consider taking photos straight over the baby, below him or her and—most importantly—at the baby's eye level. Also, intersperse some vertical shots with the horizontal shots. (Don't forget to take photos of your baby's hands and feet—what a great reminder of how small your precious one started out.)

❹ Dress for success. When taking special photos, consider dressing your baby in clothes with simple lines or solid colors. This helps keep the focus on your baby and his or her expressions.

❺ Pay attention to lighting. When possible, make sure the light is behind the camera, not the subject. If you do use a flash, find out what the flash range is for your particular camera, then position yourself accordingly. If you take photos outside, photograph your baby in the shade—simply use the fill flash on your camera to lighten any harsh shadows. (*Note:* The best time to photograph outdoors is during the "golden hours"—early morning and two hours before dusk.)

Now that you've got some basic photo tips, run out and stock up on film and batteries for your camera. You've got lots of "firsts" coming up! By following these basic tips, you're sure to have plenty of great photos that'll be cherished for years to come.

If you're looking for additional photo-taking techniques, check out Mom's Little Book of Photo Tips *by Lisa Bearnson. It's available from Creating Keepsakes Books.* ♥

Common Photo Mistakes

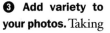

Avoid these common problems in picture-taking:

- Having a cluttered background
- Shooting too far away from the subject
- Taking photos in poor or gloomy lighting conditions
- Taking only one photo and hoping it's "the one"

Paper edge: Heartstrings by Fiskars; Photo by Jennifer Jensen

PRESERVE YOUR MOST

Treasured Memories...

Simple

FOR A LIFETIME

Your newborn's footprints, her birth certificate, special cards from a grandmother, health records, your toddler's first masterpiece, her high school diploma – all precious paper documents that, if treated, will live to tell a life story to children and grandchildren.

Protect these important documents from harmful paper acids with Archival Mist, a product that makes all paper acid-free. Economical and easy-to-use, Archival Mist forms a protective buffer against acids – the chemicals that cause paper to become brittle with time. Gentle and safe for use with all paper and inks.

Safe

Permanent

Archival Mist helps you to save priceless memories throughout your child's lifetime – from birth to adulthood.

Available at fine scrapbooking, hobby and craft stores or by dialing 1-800-416-2665.

'99
Creating Keepsakes
EDITORS' CHOICE

JANGLE.com
J
Editor's Choice

CREATING KEEPSAKES
CK OK
STANDARD OF QUALITY

Archival MIST™

MAKES ALL PAPER ACID-FREE

Preservation Technologies, L.P.
111 Thomson Park Drive
Cranberry Township, PA 16066
Phone: 1 (800) 416.2665
        1 (724) 779.2111
Fax: 1 (724) 779.9808
www.ptlp.com

Baby Steps...

Stickopotamus® Sticker Collectio

PHOTO SAFE

"Look for the Stickopotamus® Baby Steps Collection™ and our NEW Squishi

by Tracy White

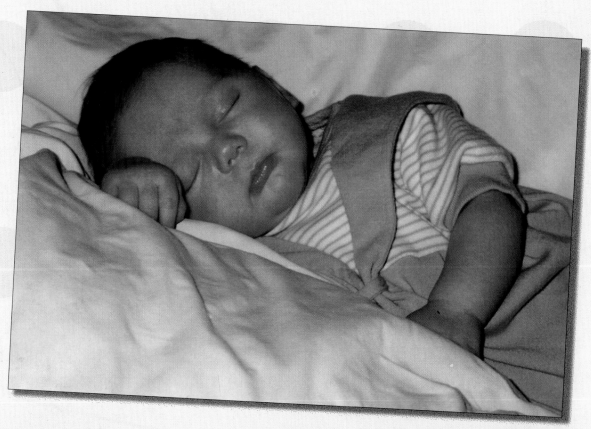

SLEEP TIGHT, LITTLE ONE

*H*ave you ever looked at a professional photo and thought, "Why don't my photos look like that?" Well, that's exactly where the inspiration for some of Jennifer Jensen's photos come from— professional photos. "I often look through magazines to get good ideas for my photos," says Jennifer, who resides in Hurricane, Utah. "I love to catch my kids in a natural setting, and I try to zoom in close—keeping the focus on them, not the background." When it comes to taking photos of babies, Jennifer offers this advice: "Take a lot of pictures while they're tiny—they don't stay that way for long!" Jennifer uses a Pentax 90WR to take photos of her three children.

- Choose pastel colors for the baby's clothing. Avoid patterns that pull the focus from your baby.
- Place a pillow under half of a baby quilt or sheet, then lay the sleeping baby on top. (The pillow helps to place him or her at an angle rather than lying flat.)
- Zoom in close to your baby and use the camera's flash.
- Try to include your baby's fingers or toes in the photo—this helps to make a great picture.

Jennifer and her son, Parker

Are you great with a camera? Send copies of your best family photos and tips to:

Parting Shot
***Creating Keepsakes* magazine**
354 Mountain Way Drive
Orem, Utah 84058

Paper edge: Corkscrew by Fiskars